MMS SUBCOURSE NUMBER 151

EDITION CODE 3

NIKE MISSILE AND TEST EQUIPMENT

NOVEMBER 1970

(REV NOVEMBER 1973)

by **U. S. ARMY**

MISSILE AND MUNITIONS CENTER AND SCHOOL

REDSTONE ARSENAL, ALABAMA

©2011 Periscope Film LLC   All Rights Reserved   ISBN #978-1-937684-92-1
www.PeriscopeFilm.com

UNITED STATES ARMY AIR DEFENSE COMMAND

This publication is provided for nonresident instruction only. It reflects the current thought of this school and conforms ot published Department of the Army doctrine as closely as possible.

READ THIS PAGE

GENERAL INFORMATION

This subcourse consists of one or more lessons and an examination. Each of the lessons is divided into two parts; the text and the lesson exercises. For one lesson subcourses the lesson exercises serve as the examination. A heading at the beginning of each lesson gives the title, the hours of credit, and the objectives of the lesson. The final examination consists of questions covering the entire subcourse.

If a change sheet is included, be sure to post the changes before starting the subcourse.

THE TEXT

All the text material required for this subcourse is provided in the packet. The text is the information you must study. Read this very carefully. You may keep the text; however, any unused answer cards and envelopes should be returned.

THE LESSON EXERCISES

Following the text of each lesson are the lesson exercises. After you have studied the text of each lesson, answer the lesson exercises. After you have answered all the questions, go back to the text and check your answers. Remember your answers should be based on what is in the text and not on your own experience or opinions. If there is a conflict, use the text in answering the question.

When you are satisfied with your answers, check them against the answer sheet attached to your exam. Re-study those areas where you have given an incorrect answer by checking the reference given after each answer.

THE EXAMINATION

After you have completed all the lessons and exercises, select the correct answer to all the examination questions. Carefully punch out the correct answer on the exam cards. Be sure to include your social security number, subcourse number, and signature. Final exam cards should be mailed in the envelope provided. The exam will be graded and you will be notified of the results. Your final grade for the subcourse will be the same as your examination grade.

ASSISTANCE

If you require clarification of anything in this subcourse write to us. Also, if you see any information in the text which is incorrect or obsolete, your recommendations will be welcome. Be sure your recommendations are explained in detail, and, if possible, include a reference which gives the correct information. Include your name and social security number. Address all correspondence to:

COMMANDANT
U. S. Army Missile and Munitions Center and School
ATTN: ATSK-CTD-A
Redstone Arsenal, Alabama 35809

CORRESPONDENCE COURSE
OF THE
U. S. ARMY MISSILE AND MUNITIONS
CENTER AND SCHOOL

MMS SUBCOURSE NUMBER 151, NIKE MISSILE AND TEST EQUIPMENT
(16 Credit Hours)

INTRODUCTION

During World War II it became evident that conventional antiaircraft artillery was not an effective defense against high speed and high altitude enemy aircraft. It was determined that a supersonic, antiaircraft, command guided missile designed to intercept and destroy all types of aircraft, regardless of evasive action, was needed. The first missile units became operational in the United States in 1953 and were deployed around vital industrial and highly populated strategic areas. This first system was Nike Ajax, which was a forerunner to the Nike Hercules and Improved Nike Hercules systems.

The Improved Nike Hercules system, with long range and high altitude capabilities, is the Army's primary air defense weapon for all North America. This subcourse covers the Hercules missile, launcher, and associated equipment and relates to the following MOS's: 22N, 22L, and 23W.

This subcourse consists of six lessons and an examination, organized as follows:

Lesson 1	Introduction to the Nike Hercules Missile and Launching Area	1 hour
Lesson 2	Missile Function	2 hours
Lesson 3	Launching Equipment Function and Maintenance	3 hours
Lesson 4	Missile Test Equipment	2 hours
Lesson 5	Field Maintenance Shops 1, 2, and 3, and Emergency Contact	4 hours
Lesson 6	Hercules Inspection and Maintenance Concepts	2 hours
Examination		2 hours

LESSON 1. INTRODUCTION TO THE NIKE HERCULES MISSILE AND LAUNCHING AREA

MMS Subcourse No 151 . . . . Nike Missile and Test Equipment

Lesson Objective . . . . To provide you with a general knowledge of the purpose, capabilities, and physical description of major units comprising the Nike Hercules missile and launching equipment.

Credit Hours . . . . One

TEXT

1. **INTRODUCTION.** Equipment incorporated in the improved Nike Hercules or the Anti Ballistics Missile (ATBM) system is located in three operational areas: the battery control area, the launching area, and the assembly and service area. These areas are illustrated in figure 1 and their functions are briefly described in a through c below.

   a. **Battery control area.** The battery control area contains the radar course directing central (RCDC) which basically consists of the following: the acquisition radar systems, the target tracking, target ranging, and missile tracking radar systems; the computer system; and other associated equipment. A detailed study of this equipment is provided in subcourse MMS 150. The purpose of the RCDC, as illustrated in figure 2, is to detect, acquire, and track the target; furnish the necessary information to the battery control officer for determining when a missile should be fired; track the missile during flight; and issue steering and burst orders of the missile. The battery control officer determines the type of mission, missile, and warhead to be used; supervises selection of the target to be engaged; and issues orders to ready the missile for firing and to fire the missile.

   b. **Launching area.** This lesson will deal primarily with the Nike Hercules guided missile launching set (fig 3), which is emplaced in the launching control area. Succeeding lessons will cover components of the launching set in more detail. The tactical function of the launching set is the prefire preparation of the Nike Hercules missile and warhead combination for launching. The overall physical arrangement of the launching area depends upon the type of installation employed. A mobile installation can be employed by a field army; however, a permanent installation is employed when the launching set is used as a fixed defense installation:

   (1) *Permanent installation.* A typical permanent launching set is shown in figure 3. It consists of the trailer mounted launching control station, three launching sections, and frequency converters or generators which supply power to the launching control station and the sections. A permanent launching section is shown in figure 4. The launching set is designed to handle four launching sections; however, the number of sections used will depend on the tactical situation.

   (2) *Mobile installation.* A mobile launch-

MMS 151, 1-P1

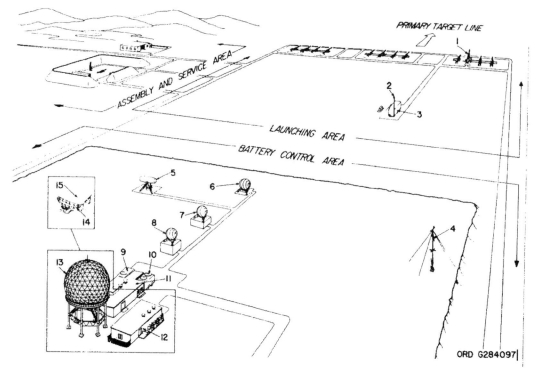

1. Erected missile on launcher
2. Flight simulator group and radar target simulator
3. Trailer mounted launching control station
4. Radar test set group
5. LOPAR antenna-receiver-transmitter group
6. Missile track antenna-receiver-transmitter group
7. Trailer ranging antenna-receiver-transmitter group
8. Target track antenna-receiver-transmitter group
9. Trailer mounted director station
10. Trailer mounted tracking station
11. HIPAR building
12. Power building
13. HIPAR antenna radome-supported-tripod
14. AAR antenna
15. AAR shelter

Figure 1. Battery layout--typical consolidated site.

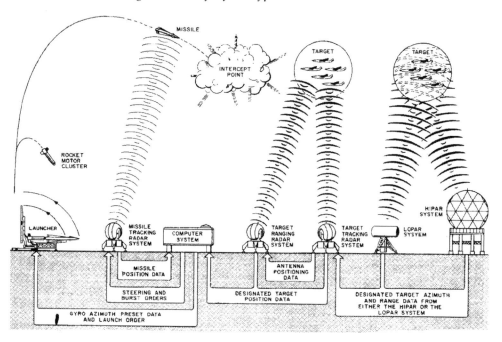

Figure 2. Surface to air mission--functional diagram.

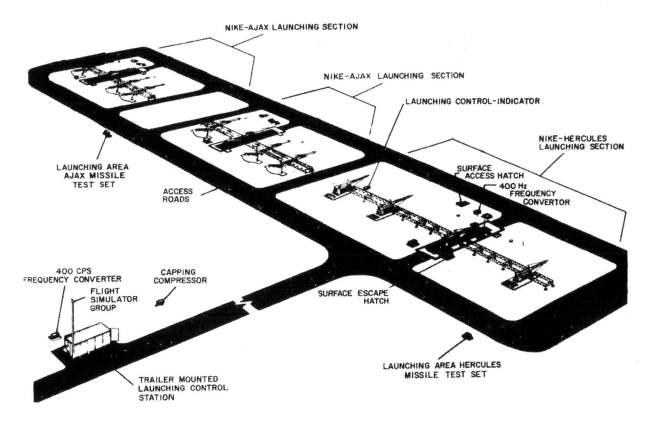

Figure 3. Permanent launching set.

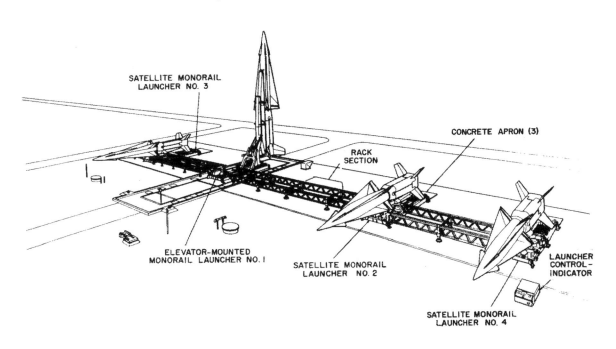

Figure 4. Nike Hercules launching section--permanent installation.

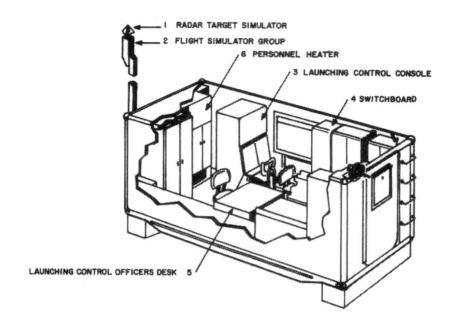

Figure 5. Launcher control trailer--permanent layout.

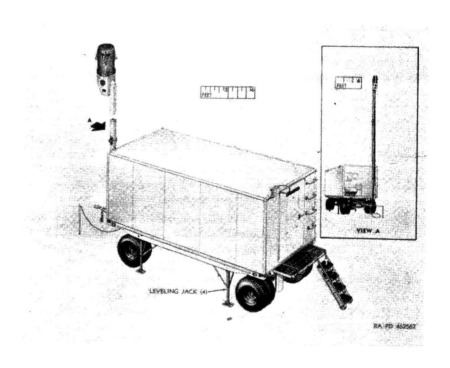

Figure 6. Launcher control trailer--mobile layout.

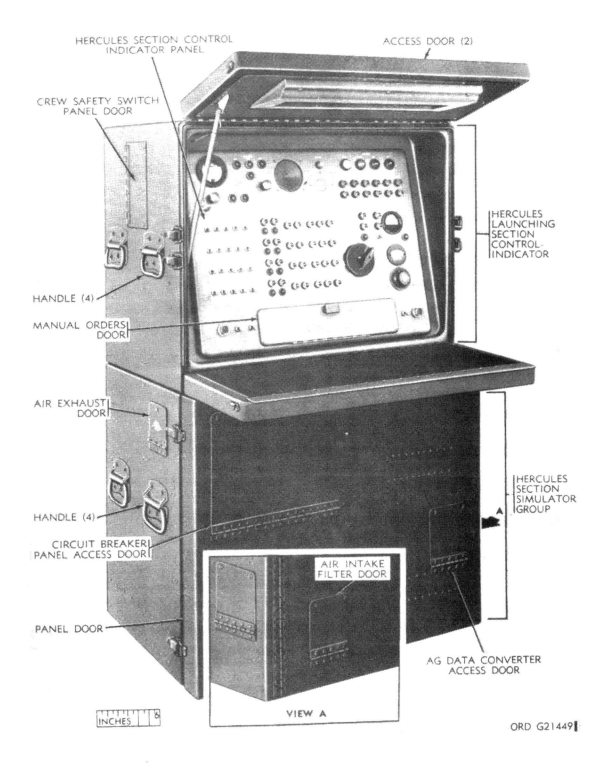

Figure 7. Launching section control indicator and section simulator group.

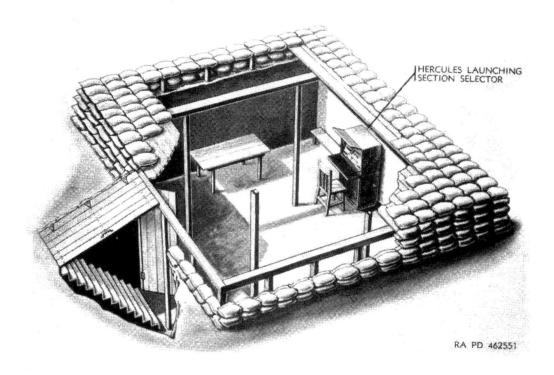

Figure 8. Launching section control indicator--mobile layout.

ing set contains the same equipment as the permanent launching set with the exception of the frequency convertor. The frequency converter is used only when dependable commercial power is available.

c. **Assembly and service area.** The assembly and service area is a support area that provides equipment and facilities for assembling, testing, fueling, and storing missiles.

2. LAUNCHER CONTROL TRAILER.

a. **Purpose and capabilities.** The trailer mounted launcher control station (fig 5) provides a data link between the battery control area and the launching area. The control station acts as a liaison between each launching section and the battery control area. In the event of an emergency, tactical communications can be accomplished through a field telephone or radio to the battery control area and to each launching section. This will permit launching of the missile from the launcher control station. A flight simulator group (2, fig 5) is installed at the trailer mounted control station providing a position to which the missile tracking radar slews and locks previous to missile designation, or after the missile has reached the target and exploded. While maintenance is being performed, the flight simulator provides a means of testing to determine if the missile tracking radar is sending proper commands. The launcher control trailer contains identical equipment in both mobile and permanent installations.

b. **Physical description.** The trailer mounted control station is approximately 18 feet long, 6 feet wide, and 6 feet high. The trailer is made of magnesium alloy and uses an undercarriage with wheels and springs for towing. The launcher control station in a permanent installation has the undercarriage removed, and the trailer is emplaced on a concrete apron and blocked up with heavy wooden beams. In a mobile installation the undercarriage and springs are snubbed. The trailer, along with the carriage, is raised and leveled with four leveling jacks (fig 6) to prevent the tires from deteriorating. The trailer houses the control console, switchboard, personnel heater, target radar simulator, and the flight simulator group.

3. LAUNCHING SECTION CONTROL INDICATOR.

a. **Purpose and capabilities.** The launching set contains four section control indicators (fig 7) that are directed from the launcher control trailer to coordinate missile preparation for launching. Circuits from the missile and launcher, completed through the launching section control indicator, provide launching area readiness information and control of the launching from the launcher control trailer. The section control indicator and section simulator group which serves as a

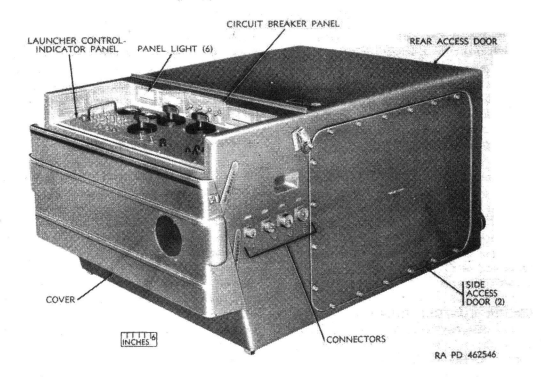

Figure 9. Launching control indicator.

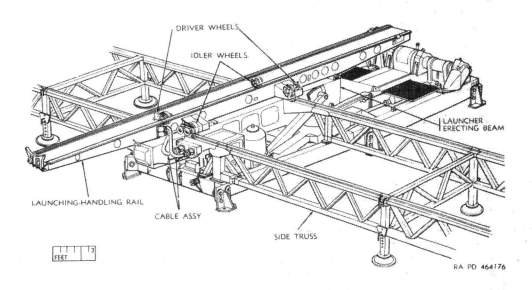

Figure 10. Hercules monorail launcher.

MMS 151.1-P7

base contains the meters, switches, indicator lights, and gyro azimuth information necessary for missile preparation. If the launcher control trailer becomes disabled, the launching section control indicator becomes the launching control center. Launching is then controlled from the section control indicator as directed from the battery control trailer in the battery control area by field telephone or radio.

   b. **Physical description.** The section control indicator and simulator group are located in the control room (fig 8), and they are approximately 5 feet high and weigh about 200 pounds each. The control indicator consists of the necessary switches, meters, and lights for the control of four monorail launchers. The simulator group contains part of the gyro azimuth circuits which will be discussed in lesson 3.

4. **LAUNCHER CONTROL INDICATOR.** Sixteen launcher control indicators (fig 9), four for each section, are included in the Nike Hercules launching set. The launcher control indicator is used for test purposes when performing checks and adjustments or maintenance on the monorail launcher or the missile.

5. **HERCULES MONORAIL LAUNCHER.**

   a. **Purpose and capabilities.** There can be 16 monorail launchers (fig 10), four to each launching section, included in the launching set. Each monorail launcher provides a means of loading and erecting the missile while serving as a firing platform. An umbilical cable (necessary to complete electrical connections between the missile and launcher during missile preparation) breaks away at launch.

   b. **Physical description.** In a permanent launching section one of the launchers is mounted on an elevator platform (fig 11) while the other three (satellite launchers) are mounted on a concrete base by six mounting brackets. Each elevator mounted launcher (fig 11) is equipped with adapter racks which permit the loading and reloading of the satellite launchers. This is accomplished by placing a missile from underground storage onto a launching rail. With the elevator mounted launchers underground, the handling rail (with missile) is then rolled onto the launchers and elevated above ground. The handling rail and missile are rolled past the adapter racks onto the loading racks and satellite launchers. Each monorail launcher (fig 12) consists of a launcher base, hydraulic unit (for erecting the missile), erecting beam, strut arm, launcher strut, and main and secondary trunnions. The handling rail and erecting beam outriggers mesh and are locked by a hydraulic wedgelock to secure the handling rail to the erecting beam. When erected, a hydraulic up-lock locks the erecting beam into position. Two stop bolts at the rear of the handling rail are used to adjust the missile into position and prevent an erected missile from sliding off the rail.

6. **NIKE HERCULES MISSILE.**

   a. **Purpose and capabilities.** The Nike Hercules missile has proven successful against high performance aircraft and has intercepted short range ballistic missiles. It is capable of performing three types of defensive missions: surface to air, surface to air low altitude, and surface to surface.

   b. **Physical description.** The missile has a solid propellant rocket engine and has a dart-type configuration with four cruciform, delta-shaped fins. The missile is approximately 27 feet long and weighs 4,900 pounds. The rocket motor cluster, which joins to the missile, is 13 feet long and weighs 5,300 pounds. The missile consists of three aerodynamic sections (fig 13): ogive, constant body, and boattail. These sections are further broken down into the forward body section, warhead body section, and the rear body section.

   (1) *Forward body section.* This section is comprised of the forward nose section and the rear nose section. They are constructed of rolled aluminum alloy, riveted to a structural frame. The four forward fins, located at 90 degree angles around the circumference of the rear nose section, are formed of cast magnesium. The forward body section contains a guidance set, a barometer probe, and four pressure probes mounted on the four forward fins.

   (2) *Warhead body section.* The warhead body section contains a warhead, safety and arming devices, and an explosive harness necessary to burst the warhead. The warhead body section is formed of aluminum skin riveted to a structural frame.

   (3) *Rear body section.* The rear body section consists of a missile motor section, an equipment section, and an actuator section. The missile rocket motor extends through all three sections.

   (a) *Missile motor section.* This section contains the missile motor, blast tube, safety and arming switch, and the necessary insulation blankets to keep the motor at the required temperature during subfreezing weather.

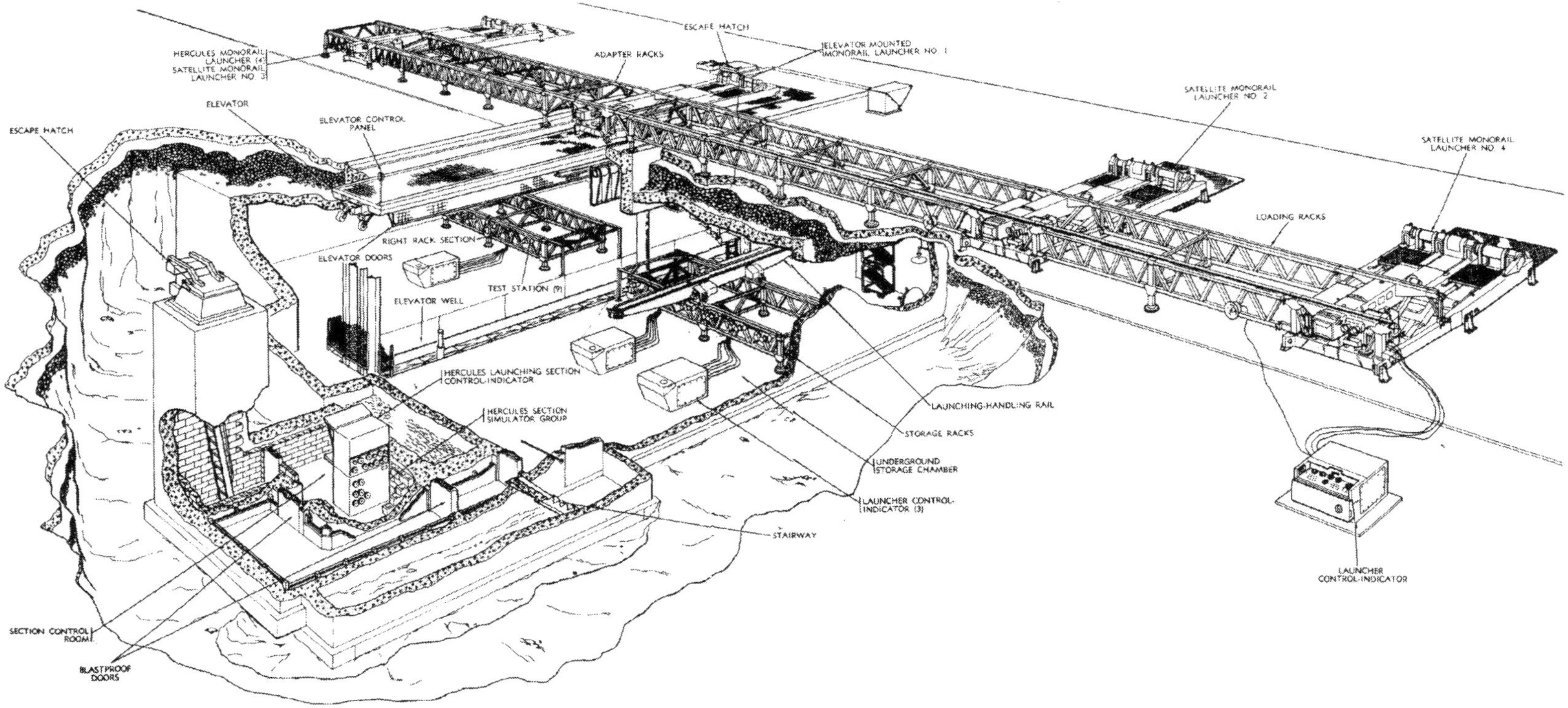

Figure 11. Launcher layout (permanent launching section).

MMS 151, 1-P9

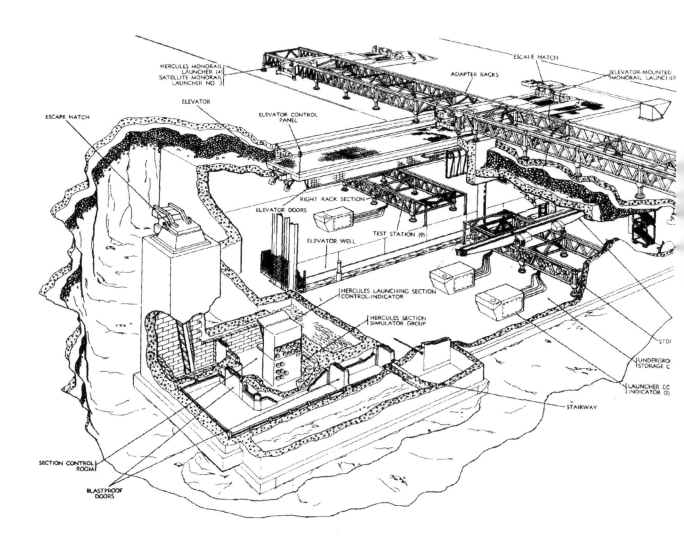

Figure 11. Launcher layout (permanent launching section)

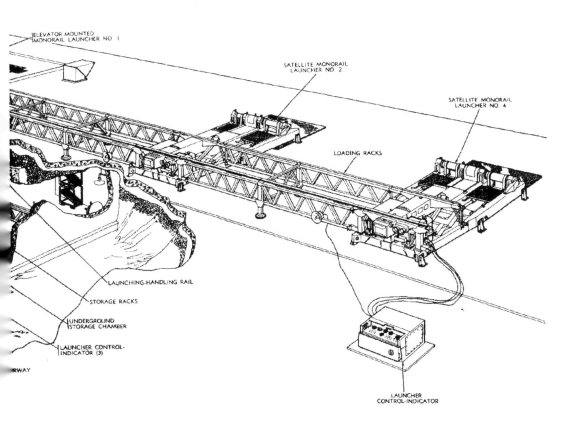

ermanent launching section].

MMS 151, 1-P9

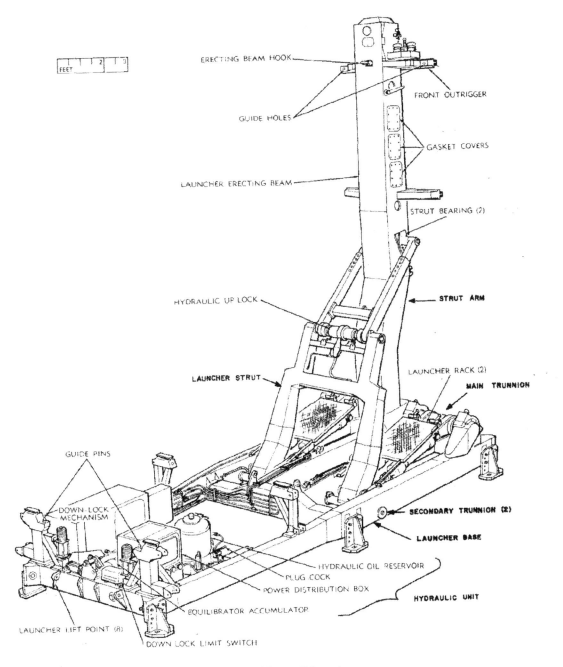

Figure 12. Monorail launcher.

(b) Equipment section. The equipment section contains a hydraulic pumping unit, a missile battery box, and a power distribution box.

(c) Actuator section. The actuator section contains three actuator assemblies, a thermal battery assembly, and a propulsion arming lanyard which activates the thermal batteries upon booster separation. The three actuators hydraulically actuate a series of mechanical linkages to drive the elevons. The door assemblies provide access to the actuator section.

(d) Main fins. The four main fins are located at 90 degree angles around the circumference of the missile body and are alined with the four forward fins. The fins are formed of aluminum skin attached to three structural members. The four elevons are made of

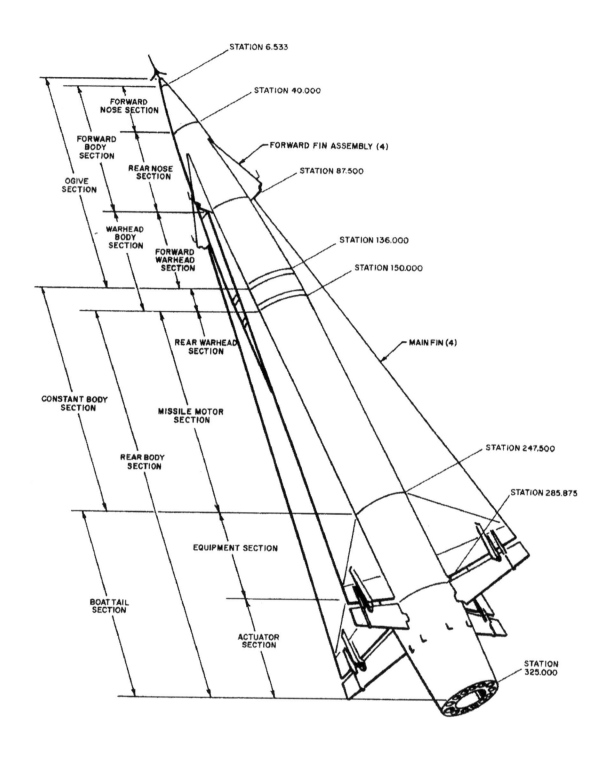

Figure 13. Hercules missile.

forged aluminum and are physically attached to the main fins to control the missile during flight.

7. ASSEMBLY AND SERVICE AREA.

a. Permanent installation. The permanent type assembly area contains the assembly building, the receiving area (adjacent to the assembly building), and the test area within the assembly building. Upon completion of assembly, test, and service procedures the missile body is moved to the revetted service area. In the revetted service area, the missile rocket motor and the warhead are installed and checked out. The assembled missile body is then transported to the launching area where the missile body is joined with the rocket motor cluster and placed on a launching and handling rail.

b. Mobile installation. The mobile type assembly area is composed of three distinct sections; the checkout area with an air-inflated shelter, the warhead area with an air-inflated shelter, and the explosive-storage area.

8. EQUIPMENT STATUS.

a. General. The varying degrees of equipment status determine the action of the personnel in the launching control area. Four equipment status indicator lights are used to determine the degree of equipment preparation for firing. These indicator lights are white, yellow, blue, and red and are normally controlled from the battery control area. During an emergency they are controlled either from the launching control trailer or the launching section control indicator.

b. White. The white equipment status is the standby condition for the Nike Hercules battery; under normal conditions, the equipment in the launching control area is not operating. During the "white status," however, such activities as maintenance, testing, and training are conducted in a normal fashion.

c. Blue. The blue equipment status is established when the destination of enemy aircraft appears to be in the direction of the battery defense area. This is the "prepare for action" status. Operating personnel "man" their battle stations, and equipment in the launching control area is energized. Personnel perform their prefire checks in preparation for launching a missile.

d. Red. The Nike Hercules battery is placed in red equipment status when an attack against the battery defense area becomes imminent. Final preparations for an engagement are completed and the missile is launched at the designated aircraft.

NOTE: Although the yellow equipment status circuit is still incorporated in the launching set, it is no longer used in the tactical situation.

9. SUMMARY.
This lesson presented a brief description of the three functional areas of a Nike Hercules missile site which includes the battery control, launching, and assembly and service areas. The main subject of this lesson was major equipment items in the launching area. The launcher control trailer (LCT) serves as a data link between the battery control area and launching area. Information required to coordinate missile preparation and direct the launching is interchanged between the LCT and the launching section control indicator. In case of an emergency the launching could be controlled from the section control indicator by field telephone or radio communication with the Battery Control Officer in the battery control trailer. A launching control indicator is provided at each launcher for performing maintenance on the launcher or missile while the missile is mounted on the launchers. The missile is placed onto a handling rail and the rail with missile is locked to the launcher and raised to a vertical position for firing.

MMS SUBCOURSE NUMBER 151, NIKE MISSILE AND TEST EQUIPMENT

EXERCISES FOR LESSON 1

1. What is one purpose of the flight simulator?

    A. Check commands generated by the missile tracking radar
    B. Check fire command prior to launch
    C. A reference point for the target tracking radar
    D. A line of sight reference point for battery control area

2. What is the tactical function of the launching set?

    A. Control of the missile during flight
    B. Storage of the missile and warhead combination
    C. Prefire preparation and launching of Nike Hercules missile
    D. Determine which target to engage

3. From which does the section control indicator receive its tactical information?

    A. Launcher control trailer only
    B. Battery control trailer only
    C. Missile tracking radar
    D. Launcher control trailer or battery control trailer

4. In which section of the missile is the guidance set located?

    A. Forward body
    B. Boattail
    C. Constant body
    D. Equipment

5. How many monorail launchers are used per launching section?

    A. A minimum of two
    B. Four
    C. Sixteen
    D. As many as the commander desires

6. What supplies the necessary power to drive the elevons during flight?

    A. Three hydraulic actuators
    B. Thermal battery
    C. Power distribution box
    D. Guidance set

7. What are the aerodynamic sections of the missile?

    A. Ogive, constant body, warhead
    B. Constant body, warhead, rear
    C. Ogive, boattail, rear
    D. Boattail, ogive, constant body

8. What service is performed on the missile in the revetted area?

    A. Electrical checkout
    B. Missile motor and warhead installation
    C. Arming device installation
    D. Final preparation of rocket motor and missile

9. Where are the four equipment status lights normally controlled from?

    A. Launcher control trailer
    B. Battery control area
    C. Launching section control indicator
    D. Assembly and service area

10. During what equipment status is the missile launched?

    A. Red
    B. Green
    C. White
    D. Blue

LESSON 2. MISSILE FUNCTION

MMS Subcourse No 151 . . . . Nike Missile and Test Equipment

Lesson Objective . . . . To provide you with a general knowledge of the basic functions of the units in the Nike Hercules missile, to include the rocket motor cluster, missile rocket motor, hydraulic system, guidance system, and the warhead system.

Credit Hours . . . . Two

TEXT

1. **INTRODUCTION.** The Nike Hercules guided missile is a two-stage solid propellant missile. The complete round consists of five major units: rocket motor cluster, missile rocket motor, guidance set, missile hydraulic system, and warhead system. This lesson will explain how each of these units function to deliver and explode the warhead at the intercept point.

2. **ROCKET MOTOR CLUSTER.**

   a. The rocket motor cluster (fig 1) is a solid propellant booster unit consisting of a thrust structure, four igniters, four rocket motors, four fins, fairing, filler blocks, and the necessary hardware for assembly. The four cruciform fins are mounted at 90 degree angles around the booster and are used to stabilize the missile aerodynamically during the boost period.

   b. The thrust structure joins the rocket motor cluster to the missile body. The thrust structure is a rigid slip joint with a tapered opening so it will mate with the boattail of the missile and lock the missile elevons into position. Relative motion between the missile and the rocket motor cluster is prevented by an indexing pin on the missile boattail which engages a recess in the thrust structure.

   c. Each of the four rocket motors in the cluster is identical and only one will be discussed. It consists of a steel head, a steel combustion chamber, and a steel nozzle as shown in figure 2. The combustion chamber contains a solid propellant fuel, cast in a symmetrical pattern, forming nine gas passages (A, fig 2). To insure uniform burning, each gas passage contains a steel resonance rod. A linear of inhibited cellulose acetate around the propellant prevents burning on the outside of the propellant. An insulating coating on the inside surface of the combustion chamber protects the thin metal wall from the high heat of combustion. A nozzle closure provides a cemented seal that protects the propellant prior to ignition. When the propellant ignites, the seal blows out and the escape of gases through the nozzle produces the thrust required to propel the missile during the boost period.

   d. The rocket motor igniter (B, fig 2), consists of 2.2 pounds of explosive — a mixture of two grades of black powder and mortar propellant — housed in a polystyrene cup. Ignition is accomplished one-half second after the launch order by applying a 120-volt alternating current (AC) to the rocket motor igniter. The current flow through the four squibs fires the explosive charge in each of the rocket motor igniters thereby

MMS 151, 2-P1

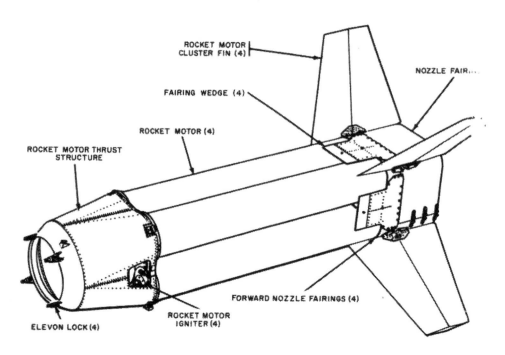

Figure 1. Rocket motor cluster.

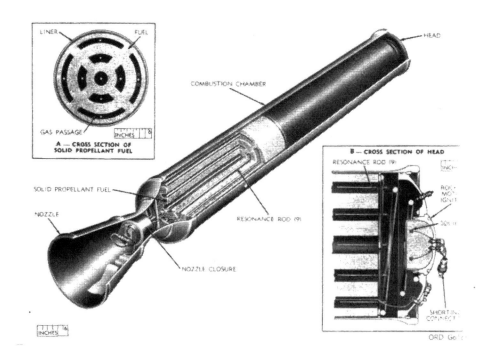

Figure 2. Rocket motor.

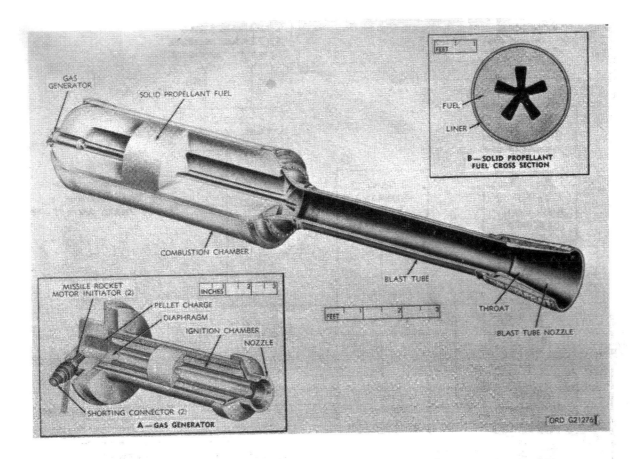

Figure 3. Nike Hercules missile rocket motor.

igniting the propellant in the rocket motors. The rocket motor cluster will burn for approximately 3.4 seconds, producing thrust of approximately 200,000 pounds.

    e.   Accidental ignition of the propellant in the rocket motor during shipment and storage is prevented by removing the igniter and inserting a plastic shipping plug in the igniter receptacle. To prevent stray voltages from firing the rocket motor igniter, a shorting connector is inserted on the free end of the wiring harness that protrudes from the igniter.

3. MISSILE ROCKET MOTOR.

    a.   The missile rocket motor (fig 3) consists of a gas generator (A, fig 3), a steel combustion chamber, a blast tube, a blast tube nozzle, and two missile rocket motor initiators. The combustion chamber contains a solid propellant grain of polysulfide perchlorate (B, fig 3), which weighs 2,196 pounds. When the propellant is ignited, the gases that are produced escape through the blast tube and the blast tube nozzle and provide the required thrust.

    b.   Firing of the missile rocket motor initiators is prevented before the boost period by a safe and arm switch that applies a short across the two initiators and opens the circuit from the voltage source. During the boost period, the force of acceleration arms the safe and arm switch, thereby removing the short and completing the circuit to the thermal batteries. At rocket motor cluster burnout, separation occurs due to the drag on the cluster. When the booster separates the elevons are unlocked and the missile roll stabilizes due to presetting of the roll amount gyro. The propulsion arming lanyard, which extends from the thermal battery assembly to a bracket on the forward end of the rocket motor cluster, mechanically activates the thermal batteries. The voltage is developed in about three-fourths of a second to cause current flow to ignite the initiators in the rocket motor. This will ignite the pellet charge in the forward end of the gas generator. The pressure caused by the ignition of the pellet charge breaks a diaphragm in the gas generator and combustion spreads into the ignition chamber. The gas generator forces hot burning gases through the nozzle onto the solid propellant fuel which burns for approximately 29 seconds. Accidental ignition is

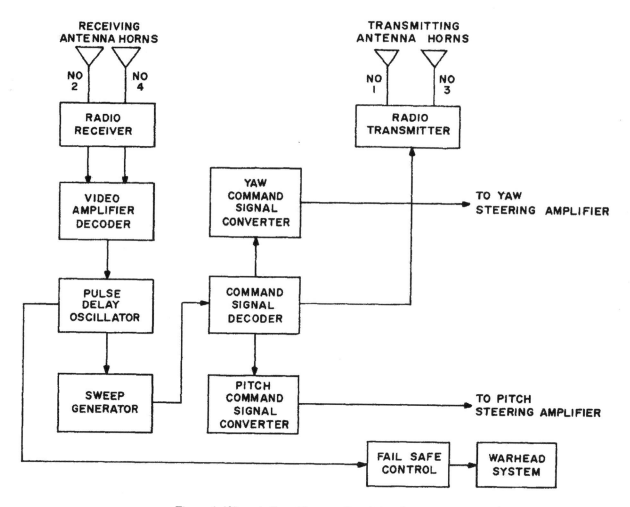

Figure 4. Nike missile guidance radio set block diagram.

prevented by a shorting connector as described in paragraph 2e above.

4. GUIDANCE SET.

a. General. The missile guidance set performs three main functions in controlling and detonating the Nike Hercules guided missile. First, it controls the flight of the missile in accordance with commands initiated by the computer and transmitted to the missile by the missile tracking radar. Second, it transmits RF response pulses which enables the missile tracking radar to track the missile. Third, it causes detonation of the warhead when a burst command is received. In addition, the guidance set will detonate the warhead (thru the fail safe system) if ground guidance ceases or if the missile malfunctions. The guidance set will be discussed as two separate groups: the radio set and the steering control circuits.

b. Radio set. The receiving and decoding circuits consist of two receiving antenna horns (fig 4), two transmitting antenna horns, a radio receiver, an amplifier decoder, pulse delay oscillator, sweep generator, command signal decoder, and the pitch and yaw command signal converters. You will remember from lesson 1 that these components are located in the forward body section of the missile.

(1) The two receiving antenna horns (fig 4) are located on the missile to insure reception of the guidance commands regardless of the missile position during flight. The antenna horns use polystyrene polarizers which vertically polarize the RF energy with respect to the waveguide in the missile, regardless of the missile roll angle. The vertically polarized RF energy is fed through the waveguide to the radio receiver.

(2) The radio receiver (fig 4) consists of

two detector cavities, each cavity containing a crystal detector. Each cavity provides a low Q resonant circuit in the frequency range of the missile tracking radar transmitter. The resonant cavity represents a low impedance to frequencies outside the range of the missile and missile tracking radar thereby limiting reception to the desired frequencies. The crystal detectors convert the received RF energy into direct current (DC) pulses. The resulting DC pulses are applied to the amplifier decoder.

(3) The amplifier decoder (fig 4) will amplify the incoming DC pulses and reject false (incorrectly coded) signals. This will prevent stray RF signals from another missile tracking radar giving commands to the missile. The amplified video pulses are then fed to the pulse delay oscillator.

(4) The pulse delay oscillator will receive and shape the pulses from the amplifier-decoder. These shaped pulses are delayed and used to trigger a phantastron circuit that produces two outputs. One output, an enable gate pulse, goes to the sweep generator; the other, a burst gate pulse, goes to the fail safe control.

(5) The sweep generator (fig 4) uses the enable gate pulse to generate a P enable pulse or a Y enable pulse, depending on the command from the missile tracking radar. The P or Y enable pulse will be sent to the command signal decoder.

NOTE: *If you have completed the Nike radars and computer subcourse (MMS 150), you will recall the missile rotates around its longitudinal axis so that the pitch (P) and yaw (Y) control surfaces are at a 45 degree angle with respect to horizon after "roll stabilization" and the missile is "belly-down." If you have not completed MMS 150, refer to figure 8 of this lesson which illustrates the position of the P and Y elevons. In this position the P and Y control surfaces do not produce pure pitch and yaw maneuvers. However, for the ease of discussion and identification of equipment the terms (P) for "pitch" and (Y) for "yaw" will be used in this subcourse as they are in the equipment.*

(6) When the command signal decoder (fig 4) receives the P or Y enable pulse in proper sequence, it will produce a P or Y trigger pulse that is applied to the respective P or Y command signal converter. The command signal decoder is composed of two identical channels. These channels operate alternately, since pitch and yaw commands are received alternately.

(7) Since P or Y command signal converters (fig 4) are identical, only the P will be discussed. The P trigger pulse from the command signal decoder will be used to determine the amount of DC voltage generated to represent the magnitude and direction of the pitch command issued by the computer. A resulting plus or minus DC voltage will be applied to the P steering amplifier. The DC voltage will be discussed during the steering phase of the guidance set.

(8) The fail safe control (fig 4) receives the burst gate pulse from the pulse delay oscillator. As long as the pulse is present, the missile warhead will not detonate. When the missile tracking radar transmits a burst command, the burst gate pulse is removed. This will allow a capacitor to discharge, applying sufficient voltage to the warhead system for detonation. If the missile guidance set malfunctions or if the ground guidance equipment malfunctions, the burst gate pulse is also removed, thereby detonating the warhead system (fail safe). This will permit destruction of the missile and prevent the missile from falling into the hands of enemy agents.

(9) The command signal decoder (fig 4) will generate one RF response pulse for every properly coded input pulse to the guidance set. The pulse will be sent to the radio transmitter and antenna horns (No 1 and No 3) then radiated to the missile tracking radar to insure continuous tracking of the missile until intercept of the target.

c. **Steering control circuits**. Due to the high altitude and extreme velocities attained, the missile encounters varying aerodynamic conditions throughout the duration of its flight. The steering control circuits (fig 5) must incorporate a positive means of compensating for changing pressures and velocities, both of which directly affect the amount of elevon deflection required to move the missile to the intercept point. This is accomplished by direct feedback from the steering control instruments to the steering amplifiers. The steering control circuits consist of seven flight control instruments: P and Y accelerometers; P, Y, and roll rate gyros; roll amount gyro and pressure transmitter. The P and Y steering amplifiers (fig 5) receive the DC steering voltages from the guidance radio set (fig 4) and feedback voltages that stabilize the steering of the missile from the flight control instruments. The steering control amplifiers convert these steering voltages into appropriate signals which, through the actuator assembly, control the elevon displacement. This results in controlled flight maneuvers that maintain the desired trajectory to target intercept.

(1) Roll control circuits.

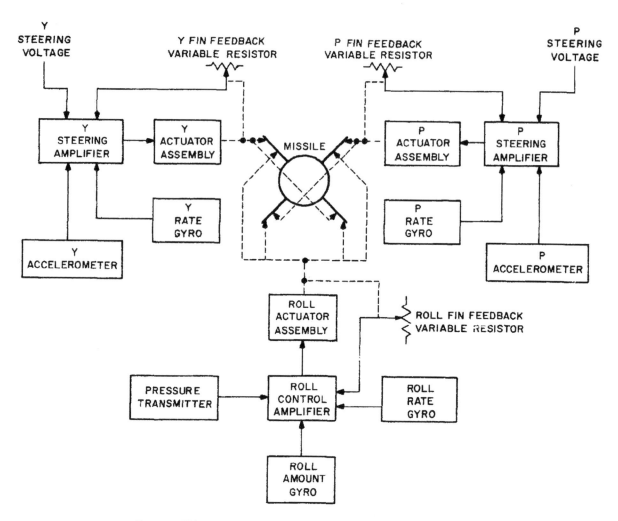

Figure 5. Nike missile guidance settering control circuit block diagram.

(a) Pressure transmitter. During flight the missile will be subjected to varying pressures depending upon the altitude of the missile. This will affect the amount of elevon deflection required, since less deflection is required when the missile is flying in dense atmosphere. (More elevon deflection is required in a rare atmosphere.) A pressure transmitter (fig 5), utilizing two diaphragms placed end to end, is used to measure the static pressure. The wiper arms of two variable resistors are physically attached to the two diaphragms. As the pressure increases or decreases, the variable resistors will provide a voltage directly proportional to pressure changes. This change in voltage will control the gain of the roll control amplifier (fig 5). An increase in static pressure causes a loss of gain. Therefore, higher pressure (or lower altitude) will result in a smaller elevon displacement and lower pressure (or higher altitude) will result in greater elevon displacement.

(b) Roll amount gyro. The roll amount gyro (fig 6) and its associated circuits serve two functions important to the controlled flight of the missile. Primarily, the roll amount gyro provides roll stabilization because it is preset to the target azimuth and started spinning prior to launch. The gyro also prevents the missile from rolling about the longitudinal axis after the missile has a "belly-down" reference in the predicted intercept plane. A variable resistor pickoff arm is physically mounted to the gyro. Missile roll movement is translated to the variable-resistor winding, due to the property of gyroscopic stability, and causes the wiper arm to pick off a voltage. The polarity and magnitude of the voltage will depend upon the direction and amount of missile roll. This voltage along with the output feedback voltage from the rate gyro, the pressure transmitter output, and the roll fin variable resistor feedback are fed to the roll control amplifier. This will increase the response of the roll servo loop to oppose

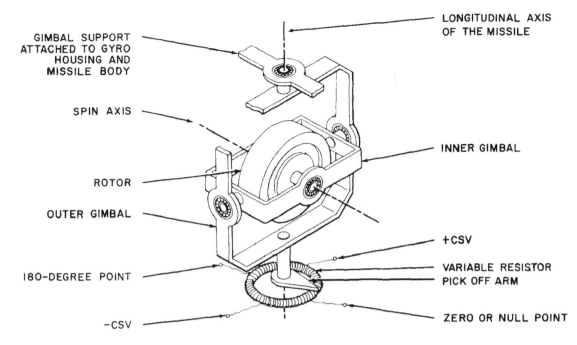

Figure 6. Roll amount gyro.

any sudden changes of missile movement about the longitudinal or roll axis. Should the missile attempt to rotate about its roll axis these four input voltages to the roll control amplifier will be used to drive the actuator, which in turn drives the missile elevons in the proper direction to stop the roll and maneuver the missile to the original "belly-down" flight position.

(c) Rate gyros. Rate gyros utilize the principle of gyroscopic precession to sense any rate of change of missile movement about a specific axis of flight. Precession is described as the resulting movement or realinement of the gyro spin axis caused by the application of an outside force or pressure. Such a force is applied to the gyro each time the missile attempts to move about the specific axis of flight in which the rate measurement is to be made; this axis is commonly referred to as the input axis. The three principal axes of a rate gyro are shown in figure 7. These axes are spin, gimbal, and input. Without missile motion the three

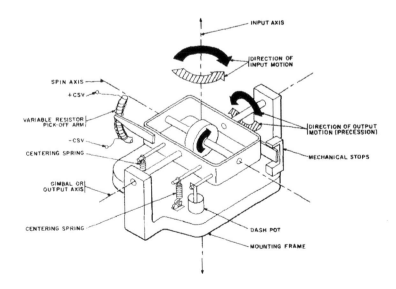

Figure 7. Simple rate gyro.

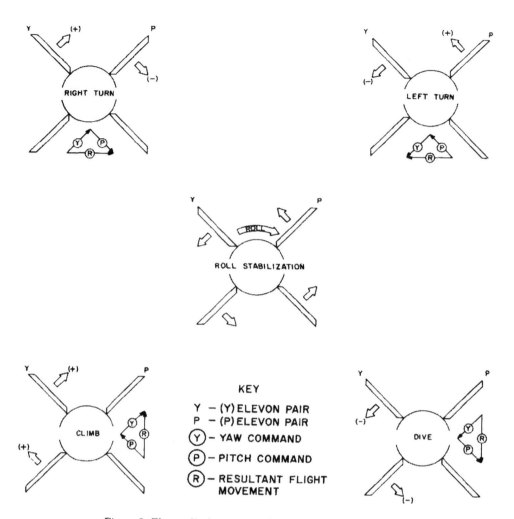

Figure 8. Elevon displacement and resulting flight movement.

mutually perpendicular axes are kept aligned with the missile by centering springs and the mounting frame, rigidly mounted to the missile. The gyro spin axis is allowed freedom of movement about the gimbal axis in one of two possible directions. Applied force, resulting from missile maneuvers, causes the gyro spin axis to precess in one of the two directions. The gyro precesses about the gimbal axis (output axis) which causes the pickoff arm to move on the variable resistor that is physically attached to the gimbal. Displacement of the pickoff arm away from the zero position and against the restraining influence of the centering springs produces a feedback voltage that is proportional to the rate at which a missile is turning. This output feedback voltage of the roll rate gyro is applied to the input network of the roll control amplifier in phase with the roll stabilization signal from the roll amount gyro, thereby increasing the response of the roll servo loop to oppose sudden changes of missile attitude about the roll axis. The output feedback voltages of the P and Y rate gyros are applied to the input network of the associated steering amplifier where this feedback voltage opposes the steering command voltage from the computer, thereby damping or restricting the rate of turn. The motors rotating the spinning mass of the three rate gyros are placed in operation during the "blue" alert status to warm up the gyro system. Gyro motor speed is held constant by a circuit consisting of a centrifugal switch and a resistance. An increase in motor speed causes the centrifugal switch to open, thereby placing the resistance in series with the motor armature. The increased resistance in the armature circuit reduces motor speed until the desired speed is attained, at which time the switch closes and shorts out the resistance, thereby holding the motor speed constant.

(d) Fin feedback variable resistors. There are three fin feedback variable resistors, one each for roll, pitch, and yaw. These resistors provide degenerative feedback voltages proportional to the

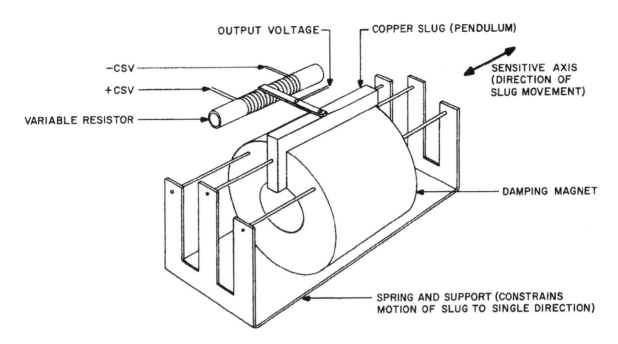

Figure 9. Accelerometer.

amount and direction of elevon displacement. The magnitude of the fin variable resistor feedback voltage is sufficient to stop the elevons at less than full scale deflection when the command is 2G's or less. Commands of greater magnitude initially drive the elevons full scale, then the other flight control instruments develop voltages that add to the fin feedback voltage to restore the elevons to a trimmed condition.

(e) Roll control amplifier. To summarize, the roll control amplifier (fig 5) has four signal inputs consisting of the roll amount gyro voltage; the roll fin variable resistor voltage, which produces a feedback voltage proportional to elevon displacement; the roll rate gyro voltage; and the pressure transmitter voltage. The roll amount gyro voltage is the primary input. The roll rate gyro and the variable resistor fin feedback voltage along with the pressure transmitter, which controls the gain of the roll control amplifier, will control the roll of the missile. If the missile rolls about its longitudinal axis, as shown in figure 8, the feedback voltage will reverse the direction of roll, thereby returning the missile to a "belly-down" reference.

(2) Pitch and yaw control circuits.

(a) Accelerometers. During flight, the missile is constantly subjected to various aerodynamic forces which are most apparent when the elevons deflect as shown in figure 8, thereby changing the flight attitude of the missile. A rapid maneuver will cause excessive lateral accelerations or a skidding tendency throughout a required maneuver. The P and Y accelerometers (fig 5 and 9), which are used to measure these accelerations, are mounted in the guidance set with their sensitive axes perpendicular to the pitch and yaw elevon plane. The accelerometers provide a feedback voltage proportional to the amount of acceleration in each plane. This voltage is produced any time the missile accelerates in the direction of the accelerometer's sensitive axis. The inertia of the slug (fig 9) causes the slug to "tend to remain at rest" while the housing, which is attached to the missile body, moves with the missile body and causes relative motion between the slug and its housing. Any movement between the slug and housing causes the wiper arm to move on the variable resistor (which is also mounted to the missile body). The wiper arm voltage is applied to the input network of the associated amplifier (P or Y), where this voltage acts as degenerative feedback to reduce skidding of the missile. Due to the mounting of the two accelerometers, their combined output is always a resultant in the lateral direction. The accelerometer feedback voltages are the largest controlling feedback in a missile.

(b) Pitch and yaw rate gyros. The pitch and yaw rate gyros function in the P and Y servo loop as described in c(1)(c) above.

(c) Pitch and yaw steering amplifiers. The pitch and yaw steering amplifiers (fig 5) are identical; therefore, only the pitch amplifier will be

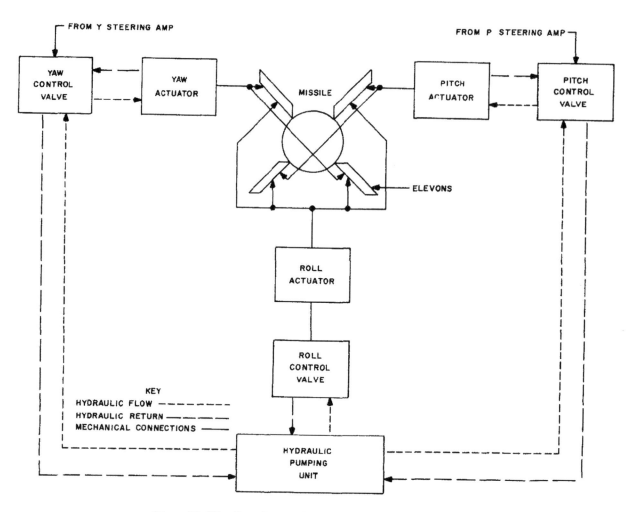

Figure 10. Nike Hercules missile hydraulic system block diagram.

discussed. The pitch amplifier is a two-stage DC amplifier consisting of four input networks, a paraphase amplifier, and a push-pull power amplifier. The four signal inputs are: the P steering voltage from the P command signal converter (fig 4), the P accelerometer voltage, P rate gyro voltage, and the P fin variable resistor feedback voltage. The P steering voltage, issued from the computer via the P command signal converter, represents the maneuver to be executed and is the primary signal voltage. The P accelerometer, P rate gyro, and P fin feedback voltages (fig 5) are feedback inputs that modify and stabilize the output of the P steering amplifier. The input network of the P steering amplifier is designed to combine the feedback voltages in the correct proportions. When a P steering voltage is applied to the P steering amplifier, unbalanced outputs are applied to the solenoid in the P actuator assembly (fig 5). This action produces a movement of the P elevons as discussed in paragraph 5a, which follows. The direction of elevon movement is determined by the polarity of the steering voltage and the amount of movement by the magnitude of the voltage. The missile responds to the steering command and rotates about the center of gravity and the P axis. The P rate gyro senses the rate of change, and the P accelerometer determines the amount of lateral (turning) acceleration. Then the gyro and accelerometer will produce feedback voltages proportional to the amount of acceleration around the P axis. As soon as the elevons are displaced from zero position, the P fin variable resistor produces a feedback voltage. The sum of the three feedbacks, acting in opposition to the P steering voltage, finally results in a balanced output from the P steering amplifier. In this balanced condition, the final displacement of the elevons is just sufficient to maintain the desired turning movement of the missile. When the missile is on trajectory, the elevons have zero deflection and the turn has been accomplished.

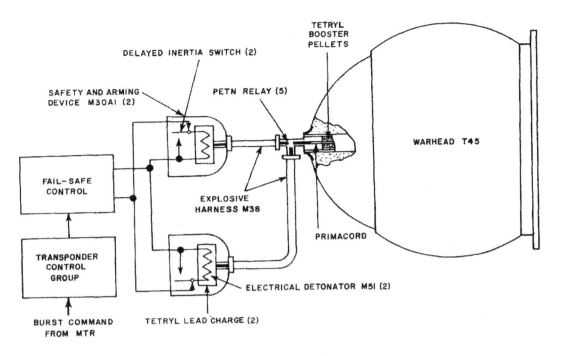

Figure 11. Warhead system block diagram.

5. MISSILE HYDRAULIC SYSTEM.

a. The hydraulic system (fig 10) consists of the pitch, yaw and roll actuators, a mechanical linkage between the actuators and elevons, and a hydraulic pumping unit (HPU). The hydraulic system, operated from guidance commands given through the missile guidance set (fig 5), positions the elevons in order to produce the required maneuver. The P and Y elevons are positioned independently by identical servo loops (fig 5) that include electrical, hydraulic, and mechanical components. The roll stabilization servo loop operates independently of the P and Y servo loops and moves all four elevons by means of separate mechanical linkages. When steering orders are applied to the P and Y steering amplifiers in the guidance set, unequal output currents unbalance the solenoid in the control valve associated with the P or Y actuators (fig 10). As the hydraulic fluid flows to the actuator, a piston in the actuator, connected to the mechanical linkages, is displaced and moves the elevons (P or Y). Movement of the elevons produces aerodynamic forces that maneuver the missile as shown in figure 8. When the required maneuver is achieved, a feedback voltage from the feedback variable resistors (fig 5) will balance the steering control amplifier. At this time, currents through the two solenoids of the control valves (fig 10) are equal, and the hydraulic system holds the elevon in position. A roll stabilization order causes a rotation of all four elevons (due to the mechanical linkage) in such a manner that any roll away from the normal flight attitude of the missile will be automatically corrected.

b. The three actuators consist of a control valve, a fin feedback variable resistor, and an actuator. The P and Y actuators are identical. The roll actuator differs only in the amount of travel of the actuator piston and the fin feedback variable resistor pickoff arm. Each actuator assembly converts electrical signals into mechanical displacements by controlling the flow of hydraulic fluid. This fluid enters each actuator at a pressure port and passes through a filter to the control valve. The oil returns to the HPU through a return port in the actuator. The control valve regulates the direction and rate of flow of hydraulic fluid to the actuator in response to electrical command signals.

6. WARHEAD SYSTEM.

a. The warhead system (fig 11) consists of a warhead, two safety and arming devices, and an explosive harness. Detonation of the warhead is initiated by a burst command voltage or a fail safe voltage. Two identical paths are provided from the fail safe control to the warhead, thereby increasing overall reliability of the warhead system.

b. The safety and arming device (fig 11) is a plug-in, fuse-type mechanism that functions as a safety device and a detonator. The safety and arming device consists of a delayed inertial switch, an electrical detonator, and a tetryl lead charge. The safe and arm switch is armed during the boost period by the force of acceleration on the inertial switch. Approximately 11G's of upward acceleration for 2 seconds is required to arm the switch. In the armed condition (as shown) the short is removed from the electrical detonator which allows the explosive charge to be initiated by a voltage (240 to 300 volts DC) from the fail safe control.

c. The explosive harness (fig 11) consists of two lead assemblies and each lead assembly contains two PETN relays (pentaerythrite tetranthrate). Detonation of the electrical detonator and tetryl lead charge in the safety and arming devices ignites the explosive harness that serves as an explosive coupling between the arming devices and the warhead.

d. The T-45 warhead (fig 11) consists of a large quantity of steel fragments arranged in single and double layers around an explosive charge and a warhead booster. The warhead booster consists of a PETN relay, primacord, and tetryl booster pellets. These charges cause actual detonation of the warhead. Upon detonation the fragment distribution is approximately spherical, with a conical dead zone in the rearward direction.

7. **SUMMARY.** In this lesson you have learned that the rocket motor cluster or booster is made up of four identical solid propellant rocket motors which are ignited simultaneously and burn for approximately 3.4 seconds, producing approximately 200,000 pounds of thrust. After the missile leaves the launcher and the booster burns out, separation occurs due to drag on the booster. At separation, the elevons on the missile are unlocked and due to presetting of the roll amount gyro the missile "roll stabilizes," turning its "belly" toward the intercept point. Also at booster separation, you learned that the propulsion arming lanyard causes ignition of the solid propellant missile rocket motor. After roll stabilization, a dive order is issued to the missile from the computer by way of the missile tracking radar, causing the missile to dive toward the target. You learned that the orders issued to the missile are received and processed by the missile guidance radio set. These orders are then sent to the steering control circuits which operate an actuator assembly. The actuator assembly, through control valves and pistons, hydraulically activates a mechanical linkage which moves the elevons. The elevons in turn produce aerodynamic forces which cause the missile to climb, dive or turn in accordance with the command received from the ground. The radio set transmits a beacon pulse back to the missile tracking radar which continuously monitors the missile position. As the missile maneuvers the rate gyro and accelerometers stabilize its flight by producing voltages which prevent any excessive maneuver. The pressure transmitter aids in stabilizing flight by controling the gain of the roll control amplifier as altitude or pressure varies. The roll amount gyro produces an error voltage every time the missile rolls from the "belly-down" position. This holds the proper reference attitude or flight orientation of the missile. You learned that the warhead can be detonated by a command from the ground or by the fail-safe control if "missile track" is lost.

MMS SUBCOURSE NUMBER 151, NIKE MISSILE AND TEST EQUIPMENT

EXERCISES FOR LESSON 2

1. How much voltage is required to ignite the rocket motor cluster?

   A. 120
   B. 80
   C. 17
   D. 6.3

2. How many pounds of thrust is produced by the rocket motor cluster?

   A. 76,000
   B. 120,000
   C. 180,000
   D. 200,000

3. When is the warhead safe and arm switch armed?

   A. During assembly
   B. During prelaunch
   C. After fire
   D. Before missile away

4. What prevents motion between the Nike Hercules missile and the rocket motor cluster?

   A. Indexing pin
   B. Bolts that are torqued
   C. Thrust of the rocket motor cluster
   D. Thrust structure

5. What insures uniform burning of the solid propellant in the rocket motor cluster?

   A. An insulating coating on the propellant
   B. Steel resonance rods
   C. Nine gas passages
   D. A liner of cellulose

6. Which event occurs immediately prior to roll stabilization?

   A. Cluster ignition
   B. Dive command
   C. Belly-down
   D. Booster separation

7. What causes the rotation of all four elevons simultaneously?

   A. Roll stabilization
   B. Pitch command
   C. Yaw command
   D. Dive command

8. What prevents the Nike Hercules missile from receiving commands from several different radars?

   A. Amplifier decoder
   B. Radio receiver
   C. Command signal decoder
   D. Low Q resonant cavity

9. What is the maximum command the missile can handle and not respond with full scale deflection of the elevons?

   A. 1G
   B. 2G
   C. 3G
   D. 4G

10. Which are used to modify and stabilize the output of the yaw steering amplifier?

    A. Y accelerometer, Y rate gyro, push pull power amplifier
    B. Y accelerometer, Y rate gyro, DC voltage
    C. Y rate gyro, roll amount gyro, P accelerometer
    D. Y rate gyro, Y accelerometer, fin feedback voltage

11. What flight control instrument controls the gain of the roll control amplifier as altitude of the missile changes?

    A. Pressure transmitter only
    B. Roll rate gyro only
    C. Feedback voltage from P amplifier
    D. Pressure transmitter and roll rate gyro

MMS 151, 2-P13

12. What does the accelerometer do to affect the function of the guidance set?

    A. Senses rates of change in missile longitudinal motion
    B. Rotates the missile about its center of gravity
    C. Measures the amount of lateral acceleration
    D. Displaces the elevons from the zero position

13. What converts the electrical command signals into mechanical displacement of the elevon?

    A. Roll rate gyro
    B. Solenoids on the control valve
    C. Current being equal in each solenoid
    D. Relays on the actuator

14. How many servo loops are used in the missile hydraulic system?

    A. 1
    B. 2
    C. 3
    D. 4

15. What is the destructive burst pattern of the T-45 warhead?

    A. Conical
    B. Spherical
    C. Scatter
    D. Fan shape

LESSON 3. LAUNCHING EQUIPMENT FUNCTION AND MAINTENANCE

MMS Subcourse No 151 . . . . Nike Missile and Test Equipment

Lesson Objective . . . . To provide you with a general knowledge of the basic function and support maintenance of launching area equipment, to include the monorail launcher, gyro azimuth, launcher control indicator, and the section control indicator.

Credit Hours . . . . Three

TEXT

1. **INTRODUCTION.** The Nike Hercules guided missile launching area equipment is necessary to select, test, and prepare a missile for launching. The basic functions of the equipment used will be discussed in paragraphs 2 through 5 below. The launching area consists of a launcher control trailer and four firing sections (in many installations only three firing sections are used) with four launchers per section as illustrated in figure 1. This lesson will also cover some aspects of direct support maintenance required to return this equipment to a serviceable condition.

2. **LAUNCHING CONTROL TRAILER.**

   a. **Launching control console.** The launching control console (fig 2) is mounted on the curbside wall of the trailer. The access door swings upward to permit access to storage space. The middle section contains right- and left-hand control panels. These two panels contain the meters, controls, and indicator lights required for mission, missile, and section selection. Through these panels, firing circuits between the battery control area and launching sections are completed. A work counter is provided for the convenience of the launching control console operator. The panel beneath the counter provides access to electrical equipment associated with the flight simulator system. In addition to the flight simulator group the trailer contains an intercommunication cabinet and a personnel heater.

   b. **Flight simulator group.** The flight simulator control unit and power supply (located in the rear of the launching control console) and the responder section (located on the extreme left of the panel shown at 2, fig 2) are the main components of the flight simulator system. The flight simulator (fig 3) receives transmitted RF command signals from the missile tracking radar and converts these command signals into monitoring voltages that control meters and lights on the responder section of the launching control console. During missile firings, prior to missile designation, the flight simulator is also used as a standby beacon target for the missile tracking radar. When interrogated, the flight simulator transmits a response pulse back to the missile tracking radar. To perform these functions, the flight simulator components duplicate or simulate many of the important circuits of a missile guidance set.

   (1) The flight simulator system can be operated in either the Nike Hercules or the Nike Ajax mode, depending on the mode of operation of the missile tracking radar. Pulse transfer relays in both the

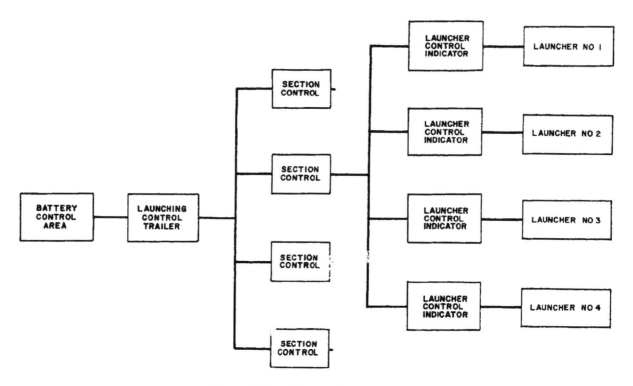

Figure 1. Launching area block diagram.

flight simulator group and the flight simulator control unit switch the flight simulator system from the Nike Ajax to the Nike Hercules mode. Transfer is normally made by continuously grounding these transfer relays at the radar course directing central. These relays may also be grounded at the section control indicator and simulator group (fig 4) with the MANUAL ORDERS - MISSILE switch.

(2) In the Hercules mode, the pulse transfer relays (fig 3) of the flight simulator group are energized. Coded command signals are received from the missile tracking radar by the two receiving antennas. The pulses are detected and sent to the amplifier decoder, which amplifies and sends only the properly coded pulses to the signal data converter, through the pulse transfer relay in the launching control console. The signal data converter demodulates the properly coded pulses and converts the pulses into a DC voltage and applies it to a pulse transfer relay that passes the DC voltage to a yaw meter, pitch meter, or a command burst light. The fail safe system works the same as the one discussed in lesson 2 (guidance set). The radar modulator generates a magnetron trigger pulse that triggers the magnetron. The magnetron then generates a response pulse that is transmitted back to the missile tracking radar.

c. **Communication cabinet**. The communication cabinet consists of a switchboard that is used for communication between the battery control area and the launching section. The switchboard has three modes of operations.

(1) In the normal mode the switchboard operator uses cable communication that is permanently emplaced underground between the launcher control trailer and the battery control area.

(2) In the wire mode the switchboard operator uses field wire that is emplaced by the using unit as an alternate means of communication in the event of a cable failure.

(3) In the radio mode the switchboard operator uses radios that are installed in the launcher control trailer and the battery control trailer. This is another alternate means of communication to insure continuous voice communication with the battery control officer for the launching of a missile.

d. **Personnel heater**. The personnel heater is a gas-operated, thermostatically controlled heater using two 12-volt batteries in series to operate the ignition system. Incorporated in the heater cabinet is a battery

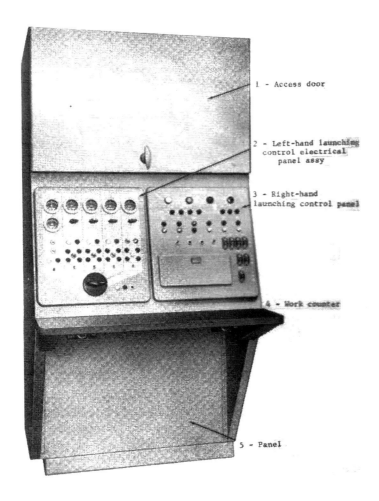

Figure 2. Launching control console.

charger to keep the two 12-volt batteries charged. The batteries are also used to operate the alert siren to notify launcher personnel when they are required to man their battle stations.

3. LAUNCHING SECTION CONTROL INDICATOR AND SIMULATOR GROUP.

a. **Section control indicator.** The section control indicator (fig 4) consists of a voice communication network, A_L resolvers (azimuth of launcher), relay panel, and the necessary front panel switches, meters, and lights for the control of four monorail launchers.

(1) Voice communication. The voice communication network provides two-way communication between personnel in the launcher area and the operator at the section control indicator.

(2) A_L resolvers. There are four A_L resolvers, one for each monorail launcher in a firing section. When the launcher is emplaced in the launching section, the A_L resolvers are manually set to the azimuth of the launcher, measured from true north as illustrated in figure 5. Prior to target acquisition, A_G (gyro azimuth) is aligned in the direction of A_L. The A_L resolver reading will be used to determine how far the gyro must be turned to reach the corrected A_G, the azimuth to the predicted kill point, and this corrected A_G is set into the roll amount gyro prior to launching. After launch the roll amount gyro will cause the missile to roll stabilize with its belly pointed toward the predicted target kill point. The corrected solution for A_G, which is performed by the A_G transmission system, is illustrated in figure 6. Example: If A_G is 800 mils and A_L is 1,600 mils what is the corrected A_G or predicted kill point (PKP)?

MMS 151, 3-P3

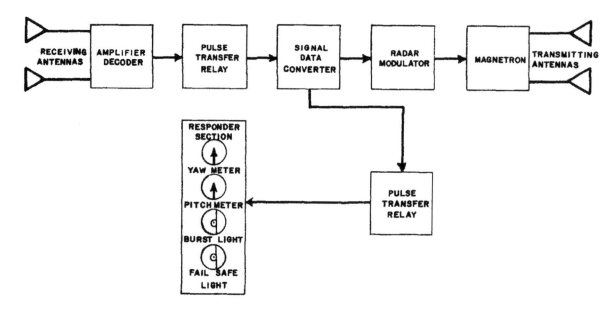

Figure 3. Flight simulator block diagram.

$PKP = A_G - A_L$

$800 - 1{,}600$

$(6{,}400 + 800) - 1{,}600$

$7{,}200 - 1{,}600$

$5{,}600$ mils

NOTE: If A_L is larger than A_G, 6,400 mils must be added to A_G since the predicted kill point is measured clockwise from true north.

(3) **Relay panel.** The section control indicator panel (fig 4) is used in the preparation, designation, launching, selecting, and the comparison of a missile and mission request from the launching control trailer or the battery control area. The battery control officer will select a missile with a certain type warhead for a certain type mission. In the selection of this missile, the launching section relay panel, which is behind the section control indicator panel, will energize certain relays if the section has this type missile. When the relays energize, indicator lights will illuminate on the section control indicator panel to give the operator a visual indication that the missile is ready for launching. The section control operator will designate the missile to the launcher control trailer, thereby notifying the battery control officer that he may launch the missile.

b. **Simulator group.** The simulator group (fig 7) contains many components of the gyro azimuth transmission system which presets the roll amount gyro in the selected missile. The A_G angle is continuously determined by the computer and is supplied to the gyro azimuth transmission system as shown in figure 8. The A_G information is transmitted to the launching set as a phase angle between two voltages, the A_G preset voltage and the A_G reference voltage. The A_G reference is always phase zero degrees and the A_G preset may vary from 0 mils to 6,400 mils, determined by the enemy target approach. Components within the simulator group convert the angle between the two voltages into a DC preset voltage that is used to preset the roll amount gyro in the designated missile. The components of the A_G transmission system are discussed in (1) through (10) below.

(1) An auto-gyro preset relay, in the energized condition, switches the A_G transmission system into the automatic mode of operation. In the manual mode the computed A_G angle is transmitted by voice communication from the battery control area to the operator at the launching section, who sets the A_G angle manually by using the gyro preset knob on a manual gyro preset resolver. In the automatic mode, A_G is sent from the computer to the launching set via the cabling system as shown in figure 8.

(2) A phase adjust variable resistor com-

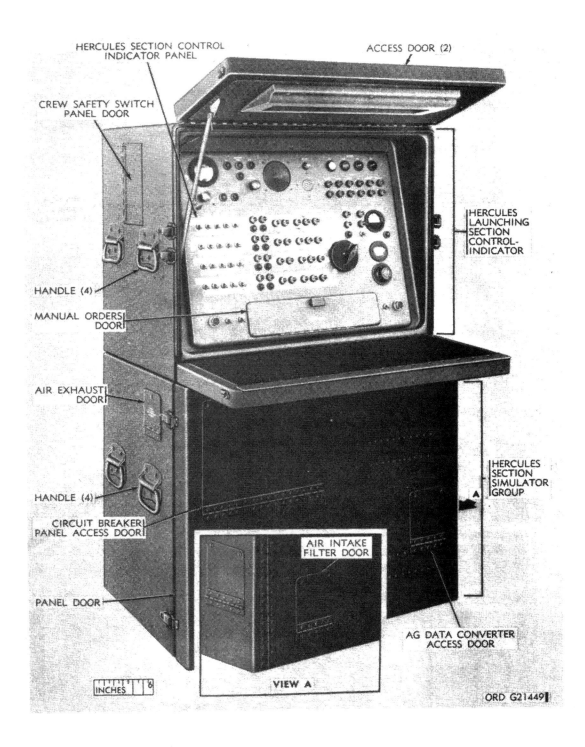

Figure 4. Section control indicator and simulator group.

pensates for a phase error up to plus or minus 10 degrees which may occur during transmission. This is necessary due to phase shift in the signal, produced by the long cable between the battery control area and the missile. The phase shift is caused by the inductive-capacitive properties in the cables. The phase shift must be

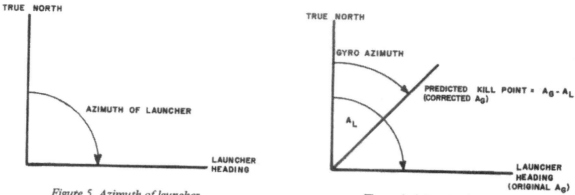

Figure 5. Azimuth of launcher.

Figure 6. Azimuth of gyro.

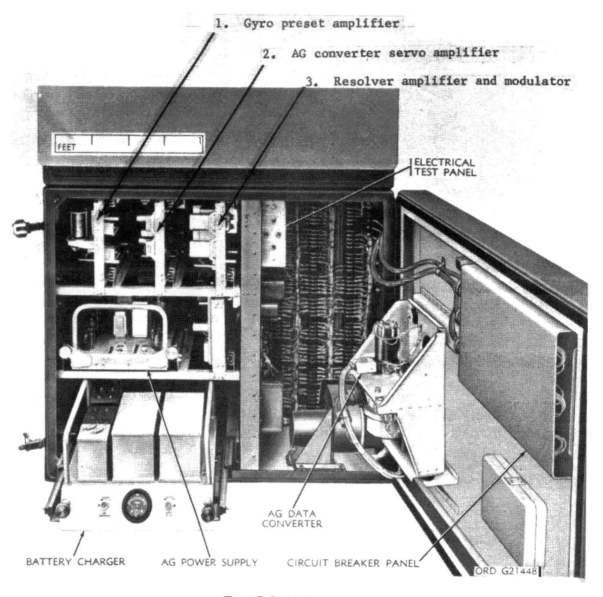

Figure 7. Simulator group.

compensated for since the A_G transmission system transfers the A_G data to the roll amount gyro by the phase difference in two signals (A_G preset and A_G reference).

(3) An A_G line amplifier, on slide No 1 in figure 7, provides impedance matching between the phase adjust variable resistor and the A_G resolver amplifier during the automatic mode of operation, or between the A_G resolver amplifier and the manual preset resolver during the manual mode of operation.

(4) A_G resolver amplifiers 1, 2, and 3, on slide 2 and 3 of figure 7, provide amplified 400 Hz voltage to their associated resolvers. This voltage is necessary to drive the A_L resolvers and the manual preset resolver.

(5) The A_L resolvers, one for each monorail launcher, supply an input to the A_G transmission system which modifies the phase angle of the A_G preset voltage to compensate for angular displacement of the launcher from due north as discussed in paragraph 3a(2).

(6) An A_G converter servoamplifier, slide No 2 of figure 7, compares the phase angle between the A_G preset voltage and the A_G reference voltage to produce a direct current drive voltage.

(7) The A_G converter modulator, on slide 3 of figure 7, converts the direct current drive voltage into a 400 Hz drive voltage that is applied to the A_G data converter two-phase motor.

(8) The A_G data converter produces plus or minus 20 volts DC ($A_G - A_L$) which are applied through the launcher to a variable resistor in the missile roll gyro package. The roll amount gyro and variable resistor are mechanically connected to a DC preset servomotor. If the roll amount gyro and variable resistor are not positioned to the correct A_G angle, a plus or minus DC error will be produced and applied to a gyro preset servoamplifier (fig 8).

(9) The amplified DC signal from the gyro preset servoamplifier is applied to a gyro preset motor. The gyro motor rotates the gyro and the variable resistor until the DC input to the gyro preset servoamplifier is zero volts. At this time the gyro is positioned to the correct A_G angle and the motor will stop.

(10) The A_G power supply (fig 7) provides the operating voltages for the components of the A_G transmission system that are located in the simulator group.

4. **LAUNCHER CONTROL INDICATOR.** One launcher control indicator (fig 9) per launcher is supplied with each launching set. The launcher control indicator (LCI) is used to provide the LCI operator local control of the launcher and missile while performing electrical and hydraulic tests. Local control is accomplished by placing the test-fire switch on the LCI to the test position. In the fire position, the section control indicator operator exercises electrical and hydraulic control of the launcher and missile.

5. **HERCULES MONORAIL LAUNCHER HYDRAULIC SYSTEM.**

a. **General.** The monorail launcher provides a hydraulic system to elevate and lower the missile for launching. Before the hydraulic system can operate, the equilibrator accumulator, the hydraulic surge accumulator, and the air reservoir, all shown on the left side of figure 10, must be externally precharged. The equilibrator accumulator is precharged with dry air or nitrogen to a pressure of 600 pounds per square inch (PSI). This provides a cushion of compressed air to absorb rapid changes in the hydraulic pressure used in the two equilibrator erecting cylinders shown on the right of figure 10. The hydraulic surge accumulator is precharged to 2,000 PSI and is located in the high pressure line to absorb sudden surges of hydraulic pump

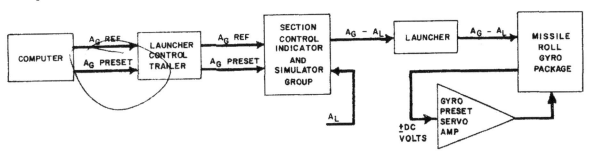

Figure 8. AG transmission system.

Figure 9. Launcher control indicator.

pressure. The air reservoir is precharged to 2,000 PSI and feeds an air regulator that charges the air section of the hydraulic oil reservoir to 20 PSI. The hydraulic oil reservoir provides a constant flow of hydraulic oil at 20 PSI to the hydraulic pump and receives the return hydraulic fluid from the system. The Deloader valve is open when the HPU motor starts allowing fluid to circulate back into the reservoir. The valve closes as pump pressure builds up to 3,250 PSI. This valve prevents damage to the HPU motor by allowing it to start under a light load. The manual system globe bypass valve is used to manually relieve pressure on the hydraulic system for maintenance purposes. It allows hydraulic fluid to flow back into the oil reservoir and must be manually closed while raising and lowering the erecting beam. The solenoid valves control the direction of flow of the hydraulic fluid to and from the hydraulic cylinders, and in turn, determine if the erecting beam is raised or lowered. The system relief valve operates automatically to relieve excessive output pressure of the pump.

b. **Launcher UP cycle.** When the launcher UP-DOWN switch is placed in the UP position, the hydraulic pumping unit motor is energized, providing 3,250 PSI hydraulic fluid to the actuating components in the hydraulic system (fig 10). The wedge lock-unlock solenoid valve is then energized and fluid is channeled to the front and rear wedge locks (fig 10 and 11). Hydraulic pressure is also channeled through the launcher up-down solenoid (fig 10) to release the hydraulic down lock assembly. This disengages the down latch mechanism from the erecting beam. Hydraulic pressure is now channeled through the restrictor valve to operate the pistons in the two power and the two equilibrator erecting cylinders. All four erecting cylinders (fig 10 and 11) will elevate the erecting beam. The equilibrator cylinders provide additional necessary power to control the up and down movement of the launcher between 0 degrees and 70 degrees elevation of the erecting beam and maintain equal pressure on both sides of the erecting beam. When the line pressure reaches 3,000 PSI, safety valve 1 opens, channeling

MMS 151, 3-P8

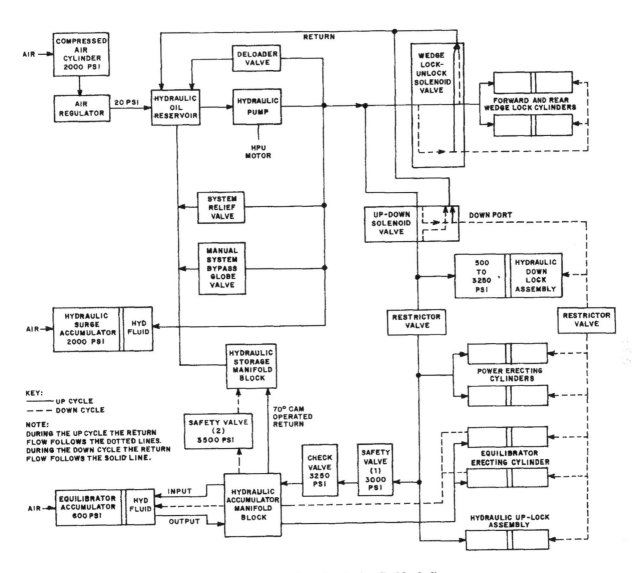

Figure 10. Simplified launcher hydraulic block diagram.

hydraulic fluid through a one-way check valve into the hydraulic accumulator manifold block and equilibrator accumulator. This pressurizes the equilibrator accumulator to 3,250 PSI and holds it. Pressurized fluid from the equilibrator accumulator flows back through the manifold and into the equilibrator erecting cylinders. All four erecting cylinders begin raising the erecting beam and missile. When the erecting beam reaches 70 degrees elevation a cam-operated valve that is connected to the accumulator manifold block opens, dumping the pressure on the equilibrator cylinders, through the hydraulic storage manifold block, back into the hydraulic oil reservoir. The power cylinders continue to elevate the erecting beam. When the erecting beam reaches the full UP position, the spring-loaded up-lock pistons in the up-lock assembly mechanically engage locking plates to the erecting struts; locking the erecting beam UP. At this point, the UP-LOCK limit switches are actuated and the hydraulic pumping unit motor will deenergize.

c. **Launcher DOWN cycle.** When the launcher UP-DOWN switch is placed in the DOWN position, the hydraulic pumping unit motor will energize. Hydraulic pressure from the down port of the up-down solenoid releases the up-lock assembly (fig 10), which releases the up locking plates from the erecting struts. Hydraulic pressure is channeled to the rear ports of the power and equilibrator cylinders, and the erecting beam begins to lower. Hydraulic fluid is forced from the forward ports of the power erecting cylinder through the restrictor valve and into the return port of the up-down solenoid. Fluid is forced from the forward ports of the equilibrator erecting cylinders through the accumulator

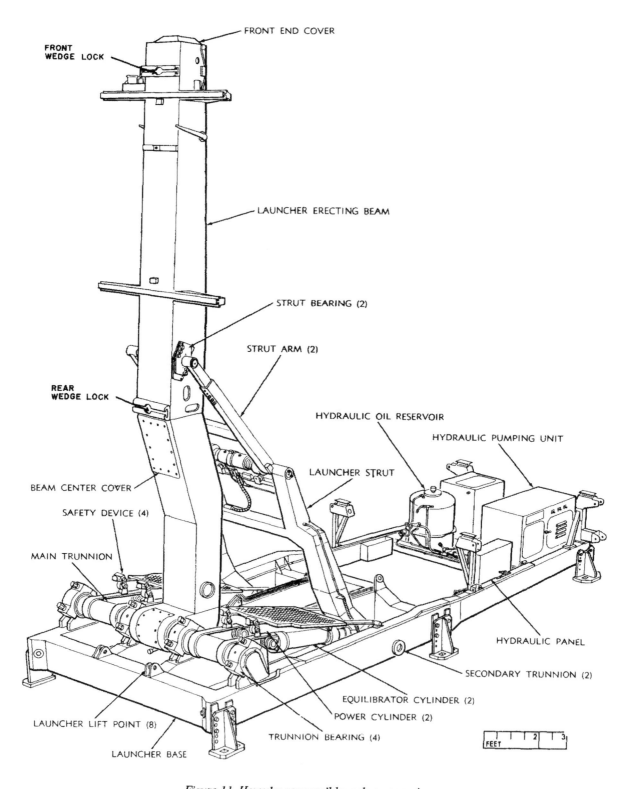

Figure 11. Hercules monorail launcher - rear view.

manifold block, cam operated valve, and storage manifold block into the hydraulic oil reservoir until the erecting beam reaches 70 degrees elevation. At 70 degrees elevation the cam operated valve closes and the fluid is forced into the equilibrator accumulator. If pressure in the equilibrator reaches 3,500 PSI, safety relief 2 opens allowing the fluid to return to the oil reservoir. When the launcher erecting beam is fully lowered, the erecting beam hook is mechanically engaged by a spring loaded down latch mechanism, locking the launcher down. This trips the down latch limit switch which energizes the wedge lock-unlock solenoid. This actuates the pistons in the front and rear wedge locks to disengage them. It also unlocks the launching and handling rail from the erecting beam and shuts off the hydraulic pumping unit motor.

6. OPERATIONAL CONTROL AND FIRING CIRCUIT.

   a. **Alert alarm.** This circuit is used with the equipment status circuits to provide an audible indication of an alert. The alert alarm circuit is energized when the battery control officer places the battery in blue alert.

   b. **On deck.** This circuit indicates that the launching sections should prepare their missiles for launching. "On deck" is given from the launcher control trailer as soon as blue status is received.

   c. **Warhead and mission request.** This circuit indicates the type of warhead and mission requested from the battery control area.

   d. **Missile prepared circuit.** This circuit indicates the total number of missiles prepared in each launching section. This information appears on a missile prepared meter at the launching control console and gives the launcher control officer and the battery control officer an indication of how many missiles they will be able to launch.

   e. **Launcher elevation.** This circuit controls the erecting and lowering of the monorail launchers.

   f. **Filaments and gyro circuits.** This circuit provides the necessary voltages to the missile guidance set.

   g. **Missile ready circuit.** This circuit indicates that the launching section is ready to launch a missile. The information is fed from the section control indicator to the launcher control trailer, then to the battery control area, and will indicate to the battery control officer that he can commence launching missiles.

   h. **Fire command circuit.** When the fire command switch in the battery control trailer is operated, voltage is applied to the rocket motor cluster for the launching of the missile.

7. MAINTENANCE.
Preventive maintenance service intervals have been established to insure efficient system operation. Effective inspection criteria must be used along with good maintenance policies, so that the materiel can be declared either serviceable or unserviceable according to operational standards. Some maintenance procedures performed on the launching set by direct support personnel are listed below.

   a. **Launcher control trailer.** When the flight simulator group is nonoperational and the using unit cannot repair it, direct support personnel will be required to return the flight simulator group to a serviceable condition. When the direct support personnel accept the flight simulator, they should require that the control unit and the power supply be sent to the ordnance shop along with the flight simulator. The flight simulator is checked out by the missile repairman (MOS 22M). To accomplish this the technician uses an RF and pulse test set group that will be discussed in lesson 4. The control unit and the power supply will be repaired by the Nike test equipment repairman (MOS 22L) using electronic shop 2, position 5, which is discussed in lesson 5. Other maintenance problems may arise in the many relays, the battery charger, and the heater control unit in the launcher control trailer.

   b. **Launching section control indicator and simulator group.** Direct support maintenance is normally limited to the replacement of relays, installation of modification work orders, and the repair of the roll amount gyro (A_G) preset system. Faulty chassis in the A_G preset system will be removed from the simulator group, when replacement chassis are not on hand. These chassis are repaired after testing by use of electronic test equipment in shops 1, 2, or 3, which is discussed in lesson 5.

   c. **Monorail launcher.** Maintenance problem areas on the monorail launcher are usually in the hydraulic system, hydraulic pumping unit, wedge locks, down-lock, and power and equilibrator cylinders. Components from the monorail launcher are checked out and repaired using the hydraulic test stand and associated equipment.

8. **SUMMARY.** This lesson has provided a discussion of the function of equipment located in the launching area and some aspects of support maintenance required to return the equipment to a serviceable condition. The discussion included the function of flight simulator, A_G transmission, and launcher hydraulic system.

MMS SUBCOURSE NUMBER 151, NIKE MISSILE AND TEST EQUIPMENT

EXERCISES FOR LESSON 3

1. What is used to check out the flight simulator?

   A. TS-352 multimeter
   B. AF and power test set
   C. RF and pulse test set
   D. Transponder control test set

2. What is the purpose of the pulse transfer relays in the flight simulator group?

   A. Select Ajax mode when energized
   B. Select Hercules mode when energized
   C. Provide local control of the flight simulator
   D. Reject improperly coded command signals

3. When does the flight simulator send a response pulse back to the missile tracking radar?

   A. Continuously
   B. Alternately
   C. When interrogated
   D. During missile flight

4. What causes the phase shift in A_G signal transmitted to the missile?

   A. Copper loss
   B. Skin effect
   C. Inductance and capacitance
   D. Resistance

5. Why is it necessary to have relay comparison in the section control indicator?

   A. To insure the proper warhead and mission selection
   B. To notify panel operator of a faulty warhead
   C. For servicing the missile hydraulic pumping unit
   D. To insure that the launcher control officer has selected the target

6. How is the radar modulator in the flight simulator used?

   A. Demodulates the command signal
   B. Generates the transmitted pulse
   C. Generates the magnetron trigger pulse
   D. Generates a trigger pulse to light the burst light

7. Who has operating control over the launcher and missile when the launcher control indicator test-fire switch is in the test position?

   A. Section control operator
   B. Launcher control indicator operator
   C. Computer operator
   D. Launching section chief

8. If A_G is 3,200 mils and A_L is 1,300 mils, through what angle, in mils, will the roll amount gyro rotate to stop at the predicted kill point?

   A. 1,300
   B. 1,900
   C. 3,200
   D. 4,500

9. If the A_G is 400 mils and the launcher azimuth is 1,400 mils, what is the corrected A_G or PKP?

   A. 400
   B. 1,000
   C. 1,400
   D. 5,400

10. What protects the launcher hydraulic pump motor from heavy starting loads?

    A. Surge accumulator
    B. Globe bypass valve
    C. System relief valve
    D. Deloader valve

11. When the launcher is in the full UP position, what deenergizes the hydraulic pumping unit motor?

    A. 70 degrees cam operated valve
    B. Down latch mechanism
    C. Up-lock pistons
    D. Up-lock switches

12. What is the flight simulator group used for during missile firing?

    A. Standby beacon target
    B. Missile calibration
    C. Checkout missile tracking radar
    D. For missile designation

13. To what pressure is the equilibrator accumulator precharged?

    A. 20 PSI
    B. 600 PSI
    C. 2,000 PSI
    D. 3,250 PSI

14. What is used to switch the gyro azimuth system into automatic operation?

    A. Autogyro preset relay
    B. A_G resolver amplifier
    C. A_G line amplifier
    D. Gyro preset knob

15. How is the A_G line amplifier used?

    A. Load for the phase adjust variable resistor
    B. Impedance matching
    C. Amplifies A_L signal
    D. Converts $A_G - A_L$ to a DC voltage

16. How much pressure, in pounds per square inch, does the hydraulic pump provide to the actuating components in the hydraulic system?

    A. 20 to 40
    B. 600
    C. 2,500
    D. 3,250

17. What is an A_L resolver used for?

    A. Orient the launcher
    B. Level the launcher
    C. Compensate for launcher azimuth
    D. Stabilize A_G

18. The phase angle between which voltages transmitts gyro azimuth from the computer to the launching area?

    A. A_G preset and A_L reference
    B. A_G and A_L reference
    C. DC preset and A_L reference
    D. A_G preset and A_G reference

19. How much voltage is required to ignite the gas heater in the launching control trailer?

    A. 24
    B. 18
    C. 12
    D. 6

20. Which cylinders are used only between 0 degrees and 70 degrees while erecting the missile for launching?

    A. Power
    B. Equilibrator
    C. Accumulator
    D. Wedge-lock

LESSON 4. MISSILE TEST EQUIPMENT

MMS Subcourse No 151 . . . . Nike Missile and Test Equipment

Lesson Objective . . . . To give you a general knowledge of purpose, capabilities, and basic functions of various test set groups, to include transponder control, RF and pulse, and AF and power test set groups.

Credit Hours . . . . Two

TEXT

1. **INTRODUCTION.** The guidance set group test equipment consists of three separate test set groups, plus a cabinet containing an oscilloscope and a spectrum analyzer which may be used with any group. Associated with each test set group are cabinet mounted test sets, a base cabinet, test adapters, cables and test leads, and miscellaneous test equipment. This equipment provides testing facilities for testing the Nike Hercules missile guidance set, flight simulator group, and subassemblies. The test set group provides a means of testing the guidance set by supplying external power and simulating the missile tracking radar system that controls the missile in flight.

2. **TRANSPONDER CONTROL TEST SET GROUP.** This test set group (fig 1) is designed to test the overall operation of the complete Nike Hercules guidance set by determining power output, receiver sensitivity, response time, burst time, order response, signal rejection, and other functions. The major units that will be discussed are the RF test set and the electrical test set.

   a. **RF test set.** The RF test set (C, fig 1) sends a group of four coded pulses, representing a specific guidance command to the missile guidance set receiving and decoding circuits. A fifth pulse is sent to simulate burst In order to generate test signals that simulate the guidance commands normally issued by ground guidance, the missile RF test set group operates on a similar time base. The generation of these commands will be discussed in (1) through (5) below.

   (1) **Microsecond oscillator.** The microsecond oscillator (fig 2) is essentially a Wein-bridge oscillator that provides an output to the waveform converter. The output is variable in frequency and can produce all the proper spacing between the first two pulses normally transmitted to the missile. An output is also applied to the horizontal amplifier of the oscilloscope for calibration purposes. The microsecond oscillator requires calibration every time the RF test set is used.

   (2) **Waveform converter.** The waveform converter differentiates the output of the microsecond oscillator, thereby producing sharp positive and negative voltage spikes. These spikes are used to trigger a gating circuit, composed of two multivibrators, which gates the coded information and applies it to the mixing and switching pulse generator. The waveform converter also generates a trigger pulse in time coincidence with the second pulse. This trigger pulse is applied to the gating and switching pulse generator to start a time base (reference) for the generation of the third and fourth

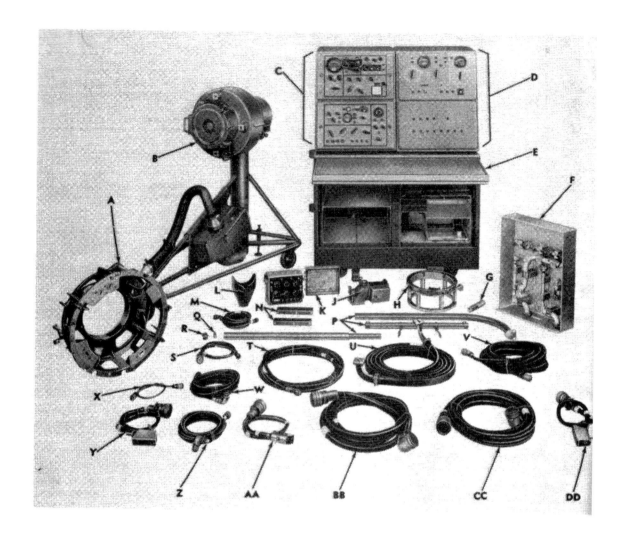

A	TA 1412–8514402 (Store in storage cabinet)		Q	TA 1206–8516629
B	Transponder control group test stand–8514412		R	Connector–9007079
C	Hercules missile RF test set group–9143471		S	Cable 1410–9144545
D	Hercules missile electrical test set group–9034602		T	Cable 1401–8514068
E	Electrical equipment cabinet–8516779		U	Waveguide–8160074
F	Waveguide assembly set–8514403		V	Cable 1415–8514579
G	Tool–9002257		W	Cable 1405–8516594
H	TA 1408–9004808 with TA 1403–9004779		X	Cable 1402–8516591
J	Transponder blower assembly–8516630		Y	Cable 1411–8514513
K	Resistance bridge ZM-4B/U		Z	Cable 1406–8516596
L	Oscilloscope viewing hood–9142994		AA	Cable 1403–9141413
M	Cable 1407–8516597		BB	Cable 1413–8514672
N	Test cable grip assembly–8013758		CC	Cable 1414–8514673
P	Mast assembly–8171229, 8171230, and 8171234		DD	Cable 1404–9141415

Figure 1. Transponder control test set group.

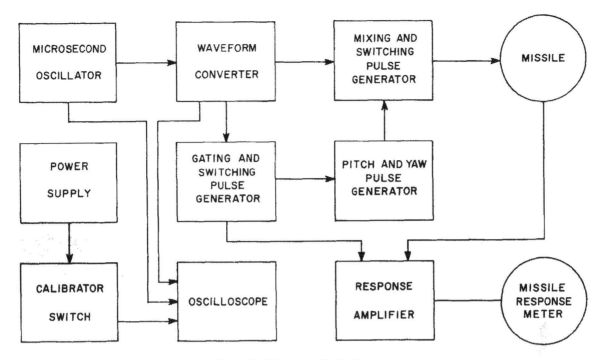

Figure 2. RF test set block diagram.

pulses. This trigger is also sent to the vertical amplifiers in the oscilloscope for calibration.

(3) Gating and switching pulse generator. The gating and switching pulse generator uses the number 2 trigger pulse from the waveform converter for the generation of a pitch and yaw command gate that will be sent to the P and Y pulse generator. It also generates a response gate voltage that controls the operation of the response amplifier and a pulse used to check the burst channel of the missile guidance set.

(4) P and Y pulse generator. This chassis in the RF test set has two command switches on the front panel; the pitch command and the yaw command. These switches send P and Y commands to the mixing and switching pulse generator where they are mixed with the number 1 and 2 pulses from the waveform converter. The output of the mixing and switching pulse generator modulates an RF signal in a klystron circuit. This RF is transferred to the missile guidance set under test by use of the waveguide (F, fig 1). These RF pulses simulate all the commands normally transmitted to the missile while it is in flight. When the guidance set is being checked by the transponder control group, meters measure the guidance set response to the commands.

(5) Calibration and measuring circuits. The RF test set provides various monitoring and metering circuits used in calibration of the test set and in evaluation of the performance of the missile guidance set. Some of these metering circuits are: the response amplifier and missile response meter, which shows the missile guidance set is responding properly to guidance commands without excessive delay time; the calibrator switch, which is used to calibrate the test set; the power supply, which furnishes voltage to the test set; and the oscilloscope, which is also used to calibrate the RF test set.

b. **Missile electrical test set.** The missile electrical test set (D, fig 1) is used to measure the input and output voltages of the missile guidance set power supplies, the input and output voltages of the servoamplifier, and the internal resistance of some of the circuits in the missile guidance set. The control panel consists basically of a null meter and switches for checkout of the guidance set. The bottom half of the electrical test set houses the power supply that supplies external power to the guidance set during checkout. During checkout the guidance set is locked into test adapter TA 1412 (A, fig 1). While in use, this test adapter is connected to the transponder control group test stand (B, fig 1), through which connections between the RF test set and the guidance set are made. With the guidance set mounted on the test stand, it can be manually moved to produce forces (pitch, yaw and roll) on the flight control instruments. The response of the flight control instruments can be checked by reading the null meter.

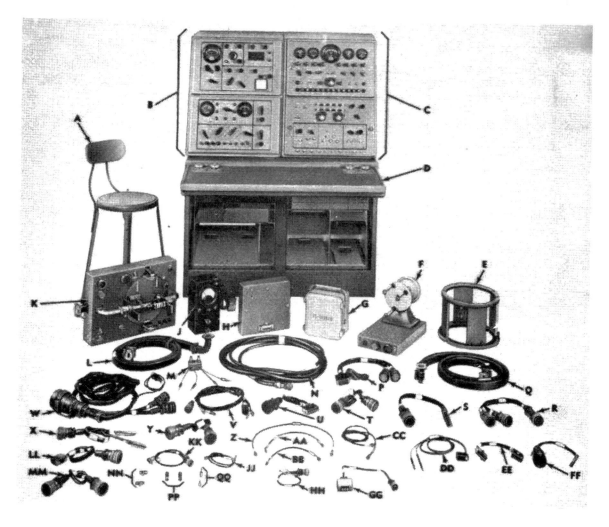

A	Straight chair—8519376	W	Cable 1201–8514072
B	Ajax missile RF test set group—8021733	X	Cable 1207–8514078
C	Electrical test set—9140286	Y	Cable 1217–8516669
D	Electrical equipment cabinet—9140085	Z	Cable 1212–8516663
E	TA 1203–8516490	AA	Cable 1220–9140462
F	TA 1202–8516730	BB	Cable 1222–9140469
G	Electronic multimeter TS-505D/U	CC	Cable 1213–8516664
H	TA 1201–8516480	DD	Cable 1211–8516662
J	Electronic voltmeter ME-6/U	EE	Cable 1221–9140501
K	TA 1204–9136059	FF	Cable 1206–8514077
L	Waveguide—9004735	GG	Cable 1209–8514085
M	TA 1205–8514628	HH	Cable 1215–8516667
N	Cable 1210–8516661	JJ	Cable 1218–8155317
P	Cable 1223–9140506	KK	Cable 1214–8516666
Q	Waveguide—9004598	LL	Cable 1208–8514079
R	Cable 1224–9140527	MM	Cable 1216–8516668
S	Cable 1204–8514075	NN	Adapter connector UG-274A/U
T	Cable 1225–9140498	PP	Adapter connector UG-1090/U
U	Cable 1203–8514074	QQ	TA 1206–8516629
V	Cable 1226–9140467		

Figure 3. RF and pulse components test set group.

3. **RF AND PULSE COMPONENTS TEST SET GROUP.**

   a. **General.** The RF and pulse components test set group (fig 3) consists of the Ajax missile RF test set (B, fig 3), the electrical test set (C, fig 3), the electrical equipment cabinet (D, fig 3), cables, adapters, and other associated test equipment. The lower part of the electrical equipment cabinet houses all the unmounted items of test equipment shown in figure 3. This test set group is designed to test RF and pulse components (chassis or modules) that are removable from the Nike Hercules or Nike Ajax guidance set.

   b. **Nike Ajax test set.** This test set is similar to the Nike Hercules test set discussed in paragraph 2a above and will not be discussed in this lesson.

   c. **Electrical test set.** The assemblies comprising the electrical test set (C, fig 3) are the electrical equipment cabinet, the upper electrical equipment drawer, and the lower electrical equipment drawer. The upper drawer contains the power supplies necessary for operation of the units under test and the chassis contained in the lower drawer. The lower drawer contains the pulse forming chassis used in performing tests on various pulse components of the missile guidance set.

   (1) Upper equipment drawer. The upper equipment drawer contains seven plug-in units, mounted in a framework. The plug-in units are discussed in (a) through (f) below.

   (a) The AC power supply (fig 4) produces regulated 120 volts, 1,700 Hz and 45 volts, 200 Hz from a -28 volt input. The regulated 120-volt, 1,700-Hz uses a transistorized series regulator. The 45-volt, 200-Hz uses an autotransformer, a vibrator, and associated filters.

   (b) The -100 and +150-volt power supply furnishes regulated -100 and +150-volt outputs to other components of the electrical test set and to units under test. In addition, the power supply uses a -150-volt from the -150 and +250-volt regulated power supply to furnish a regulated -60-volt output to units of the electrical test set and to units under test.

   (c) The -150 and +250-volt power supply furnishes regulated -150 and +240-volt outputs. It also furnishes unfiltered and unregulated +240 volts to other components of the electrical test set and units under test.

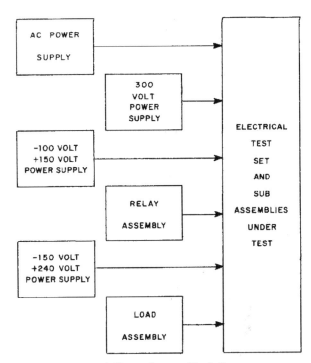

Figure 4. Upper drawer–block diagram.

   (d) The 300-volt power supply contains two +300-volt regulated DC supplies and is the source of the 6.3-volt AC heater voltage for the circuits in the upper drawer.

   (e) The relay assembly provides power to various chassis of the electrical test set and to the units under test. The relays are activated by the TEST-POWER switch on the electrical test set front panel (C, fig 3).

   (f) The load assembly provides load resistors for various Nike Hercules missile guidance set components under test. Shunts are also provided for meters of the RF and pulse components test set group.

   (2) Lower equipment drawer. The lower electrical equipment drawer contains 10 plug-in units that will be discussed in (a) through (g) below.

   (a) The pulse generator (fig 5) is basically a multivibrator with two modes of operation, monostable or free running, either of which can be selected by a selector switch on the front of the lower drawer. The pulse generator generates synchronizing pulses at variable repetition rates which are applied to a 5-microsecond pulse generator, a 0.25-microsecond pulse generator, and a variable width pulse generator.

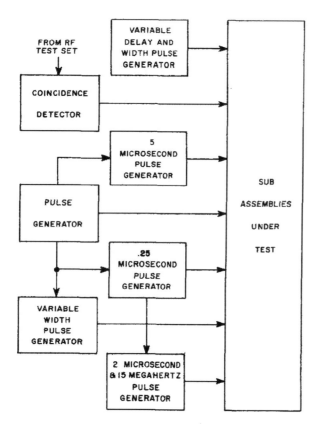

Figure 5. Lower drawer--block diagram.

(b) The 5-microsecond pulse generator supplies alternate pitch and yaw pulses (positive and negative) and a burst pulse to the units under test. This is accomplished by using trigger amplifiers, multivibrators, and blocking oscillators.

(c) The 0.25 microsecond pulse generator is made up of two identical four-stage pulse generators consisting of a cathode follower input stage, a blocking oscillator, and two stages of amplification. The output pulses are used to furnish pulses to the electrical test set and to units under test.

(d) The variable width pulse generator receives pulses of various widths and amplitudes and generates positive and negative pulses with various widths and amplitudes to be used to test components of the Nike Hercules guidance set. These pulses are controlled by the function switch on the front of the lower drawer.

(e) The coincidence detector receives a signal pulse train from the missile RF test set and furnishes undelayed, delayed, and decoded outputs for use in testing the RF and pulse components of the missile guidance set.

(f) The variable delay and width pulse generator contains two phantastron circuits. One phantastron is designed to produce a pulse that is variable in width and the other produces a pulse whose time of generation is variable. These pulses are applied to various units under test.

(g) The 2 microsecond and 15 megahertz pulse generator receives a trigger from the .25 microsecond pulse generator and produces pulses used for testing the command detonation circuits. The .25 microsecond input also triggers a ringer or shock excite oscillator. The ringer generates a 15 megahertz pulse, .25 microseconds wide, that is used for testing the RF detector.

(3) Missile guidance set test adapters.

(a) General. There are many test adapters shown in figures 1 and 3. They are used to check out the missile guidance set. Some of the major test adapters are discussed in (b) through (f) below.

(b) Adapter 1201 (W, fig 3). The adapter is used in testing signal data converters of the guidance set. The test adapter provides connection between the test equipment and the unit under test.

(c) Adapter 1202 (F, fig 3). The adapter is used in testing units from the Nike Ajax missile guidance set, to include steering order demodulators and signal data converters.

(d) Adapter 1204 (K, fig 3). The adapter is used in testing beacons, receiver-transmitter and radar modulators.

(e) Adapter 1207 (X, fig 3). The adapter is used to test vane axial fans of the guidance missile flight simulator.

(f) Adapter 1211 (DD, fig 3). The adapter is used to test amplifier decoders, delay line radio receivers, RF detectors, and pulse delay network

4. AF AND POWER COMPONENTS TEST SET.

a. **General.** The AF and power components test set group (fig 6) is designed to test audiofrequency and power components (modules or chassis) within the Nike

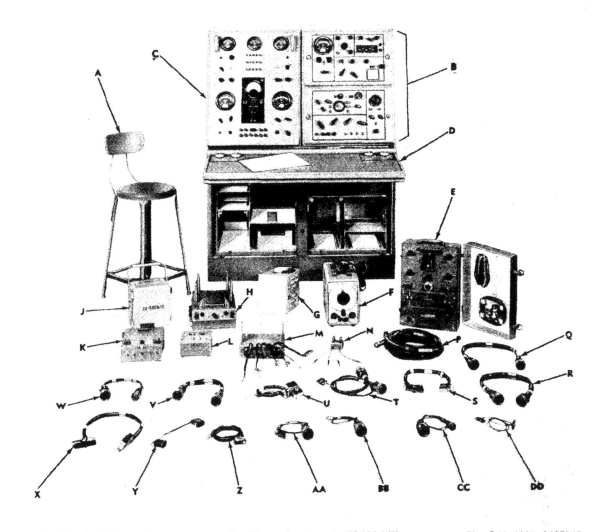

A	Straight chair—8519376	J	Electronic multimeter TS-505 D/U	U	Cable 1305–9137867
B	Hercules missile RF test set group—9153471	K	TA 1302–8159342	V	Cable 1308–9149046
		L	TA 1304–8516830	W	Cable 1310–8516769
C	Electrical test set—9138293	M	TA 1303–8516820	X	Cable 1303–9137868
D	Electrical equipment cabinet—9140121	N	TA 1305–9137867	Y	Cable 1311–8516843
		P	Cable 1301–8514067	Z	Cable 1302–8514069
E	Electrical test set—9005609	Q	Cable 1312–8516938	AA	Cable 1306–8516764
F	Signal generator—9024903	R	Cable 1307–8516766	BB	Cable 1309–8516768
G	Oscilloscope AN/USM-32	S	Cable 1304–8516762	CC	Cable 1313–9136026
H	TA 1301–9140126	T	Cable 1318–9158772	DD	Cable 1317–9158754

Figure 6. AF and power components test set group.

Hercules missile guidance set. The RF test set (B, fig 6) will also be used with the RF and pulse components test set group (fig 3). Therefore, these two test set groups (fig 3 and 6) must be placed adjacent to each other to permit cabling between the two test set groups. Tests made at this position include DC voltage and current measurements, DC amplifier output current measurements, resistance measurements, and command and fail safe circuit measurements.

b. **Electrical test set.** The electrical test set (C, fig 6) provides power supply circuits, resistive loads, and metering circuits used in making acceptance tests on units tested with the AF and power test set group. The electrical test set is composed of an electrical test panel and subassemblies, all housed within the electrical cabinet. All operating controls, meters, external adjustments, and fuses used while tests are being made are mounted on the sloping front of the test panel. A

MMS 151, 4-P7

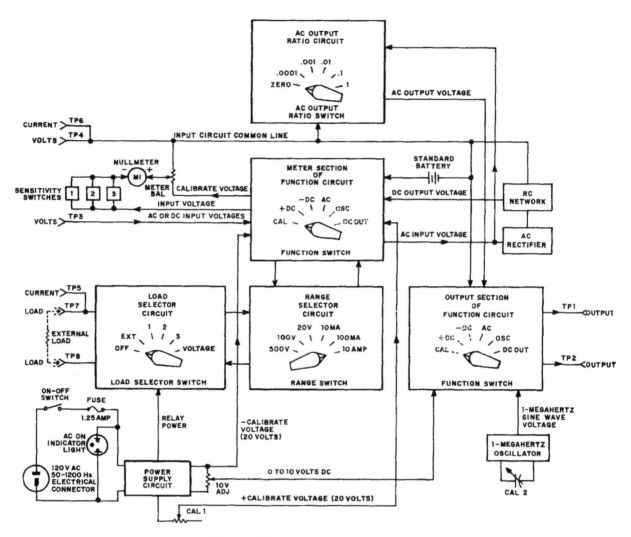

Figure 7. Electrical test set--block diagram.

work surface is provided by folding the door to the electrical equipment cabinet (fig 6) up into position. Located on the shelf are circuit connectors with associated test points which provide electrical connectors to units under test and test equipment.

c. **Electrical test set (9005609).**

(1) General. This test set (E, fig 6) is used to confirm the accuracy of high frequency sine waves, meters, and AC and DC power sources within the guidance set test equipment. A calibration team should calibrate this test set every 90 days. The instrument is then used by Nike support maintenance personnel to make regularly scheduled comparison checks to determine the accuracy of other test equipment and power supplies. The test set is also used in malfunction isolation. The test set contains a 1-megahertz crystal oscillator, which supplies a reference signal used in making frequency checks, and a standard battery, used to check the output of internal power supplies.

(2) Power supply circuit. A block diagram of the test set is shown in figure 7. The internal power supply operates from 120 volts AC, 50 Hz to 1.2 KHz. When the ON-OFF switch is closed, AC ON indicator light illuminates and power is applied to the power supply. The power supply produces relay power which is applied to the load selector circuit to condition relays for an external load. Another voltage produced is the 0 to 10 volt which is used to compare with the standard battery voltage. Finally, the power supply produces a 20-volt calibrate voltage which is applied to the function circuit.

(3) Calibration. Before each use, the

maintenance technician should check the standard battery to see that it was calibrated by a calibration team within the past 90 days. The voltage output of the standard battery is recorded on the battery by the calibration team and is normally near 10 volts. With the FUNCTION switch (fig 7) in the CAL position, the standard battery voltage is applied to one side of the null meter while the plus calibrate voltage is applied to the other side and CAL 1 variable resistor is adjusted for a zero reading on the null meter. This calibrates the test set.

(4) Meter circuit. Input voltages to be measured are applied to TP3 (fig 7), through the meter section of the FUNCTION switch, through three pushbutton SENSITIVITY switches, to one side of the null meter. Each of the three SENSITIVITY switches provides a different resistive input network to the meter and switch 3 gives maximum meter sensitivity. A calibrate voltage from the power supply is applied to the other side of the null meter through the meter BAL variable resistor. The meter BAL resistor contains a calibrated dial. This dial is adjusted until the meter is balanced (reads zero) and the voltage measured is determined from the dial setting.

(5) Range selector circuits. This circuit consists of a six-position switch (fig 7) and associated voltage dropping resistors. It functions along with the load selector to provide the correct circuit path to the null meter. When voltage is measured, the dropping resistors supply only a portion of the input to the meter. For current measurements, additional resistors are added into the circuits by the LOAD SELECTOR switch.

(6) Load selector circuit. The load selector circuit (fig 7) operates in conjunction with the range selector to provide the correct circuit path and resistive load for the selected current range. The current to be measured is applied to TP5 and TP6. Positions 1, 2, and 3 correspond to positions 10 ma, 100 ma, and 10 amp of the range selector which determines the maximum current that can be measured with the null meter. The VOLTAGE position is used when measuring voltage and EXT position is used for connecting an external current at TP7 and TP8. When placed to OFF, the switch breaks all voltage and current circuits to the null meter.

(7) Function circuit. This circuit is divided into a meter section and an output section. The meter section provides various connections to the null meter, while the output section provides output circuit connections to TP1 and TP2. In the CAL position, the standard battery and pulse calibrate voltages are applied to opposite sides of the null meter as described in c(3) above. The calibrate voltage polarity, fed to the null meter from the power supply, may be changed (plus or minus DC positions). This permits measurement of any polarity DC voltage applied between TP3 and TP4. The AC position of this switch applies the AC input voltage to a rectifier circuit. The rectified AC is filtered to a smooth DC voltage and applied through the SENSITIVITY switches to one side of the null meter. The plus or minus calibrate voltage is applied to the other side of the null meter and the meter BAL resistor is adjusted to null (zero) the meter. The effective value of the AC voltage is read from the meter BAL dial. The AC voltage is also applied to the AC output ratio circuit where a percentage of the AC is applied to the output section of the FUNCTION switch. This percentage of the AC voltage is present between TP1 and TP2 when the switch is in the AC position. The OSC position of the FUNCTION switch applies the 1-MHz sine wave between TP1 and TP2. The CAL 2 capacitor adjustment is used to calibrate the 1-MHz sine wave. The DC OUT position completes the circuit path from the 0- to 10-volt supply to TP1 and TP2 output binding posts. This voltage is adjustable from 0 to 10 volts by the 10-volt ADJ resistor.

d. **Cables and test adapters.** The various meters, cables, and test adapters listed in figures 1, 3, and 6 are used in making connections to the units being tested and the test equipment. Some of these are stored in the cabinet shown in figure 8.

5. OSCILLOSCOPE AND SPECTRUM ANALYZER.

a. **General.** The oscilloscope and spectrum analyzer electrical cabinet (fig 9) is not used to perform complete tests by itself but is used as supplementary equipment with any of the test set groups. The test set group consists of oscilloscope AN/USM-50A and spectrum analyzer TS-148/UP which are used to provide visual indications of outputs of the unit under test.

b. **Oscilloscope.** The oscilloscope (fig 9) is a general purpose broadband test instrument. It operates from a line voltage of 103 to 127 volts at a frequency of 50 to 1,000 Hertz. Signal input sensitivity without an attenuation probe is 10 millivolts per centimeter. Maximum signal input is 450 volts with the attenuation probe which has an attenuation ratio of 10 to 1. The nominal bandwidth is 5 Hz to 15 MHz; sine waves from 3 Hz to 20 MHz may be synchronized. A calibration dial, graduated from 10 to 100 millivolts, is used to measure amplitude. Time markers are supplied by a pulse forming assembly at 0.2, 1.5, 20, 100, 500, and

A	Storage cabinet—8514663	G	TA 1210—9136290
B	TA 1209—9137846	H	TA 1309—9158734
C	TA 1412—8514402	J	TA 1211—9137822
D	TA 1306—9158718	K	TA 1207—9137715
E	AC-DC voltmeter—9158763 (with case)	L	TA 1208—9137723
		M	TA 1212—9138106
F	TA 1307—9138008	N	Instruction cards

Figure 8. Storage cabinet and equipment.

2,000 microsecond intervals. The sweep time is continuously adjustable from 0.7 microseconds per centimeter to 0.015 second per centimeter in five bands. A jack is provided to supply an external sync for triggering the sweep. A built-in trigger provides +25-volt, 1.5-microsecond pulses with a rise time of 0.15 microsecond at a repetition rate of 10 Hz to 10 KHz.

c. **Spectrum analyzer.** The spectrum analyzer (fig 9) is a general purpose test set designed for testing the overall system performance of a radar system. It checks the frequency of signal generators, local oscillators, magnetrons, and transmit-receive (TR) and antitransmit-receive (ATR) boxes. In addition, it measures pulse width, radiofrequency spectrum width, and the quality (Q) of resonant cavities. All signals and spectrum measurements are displayed on a built-in 3-inch cathode-ray oscilloscope screen. The frequencies of the frequency meter and the signal generator are read directly from a calibrated dial.

6. **SUMMARY.** This lesson has presented a discussion of the test set groups which are used to troubleshoot and repair many of the components and assemblies taken from the missile or found in the launching area. These included the transponder control test set group which is used to determine the overall operation of the guidance set, the RF and pulse components test set group which is used to test and repair chassis or modules that are removable from the guidance set, the AF and power components test set which is also used to test chassis or modules from the guidance set. However, chassis tested at this test set operate in the DC to audio frequency range. Finally, this lesson discussed the oscilloscope and spectrum analyzer which supplements the test set groups and facilitates further analysis of operation of units tested at any of the test set groups.

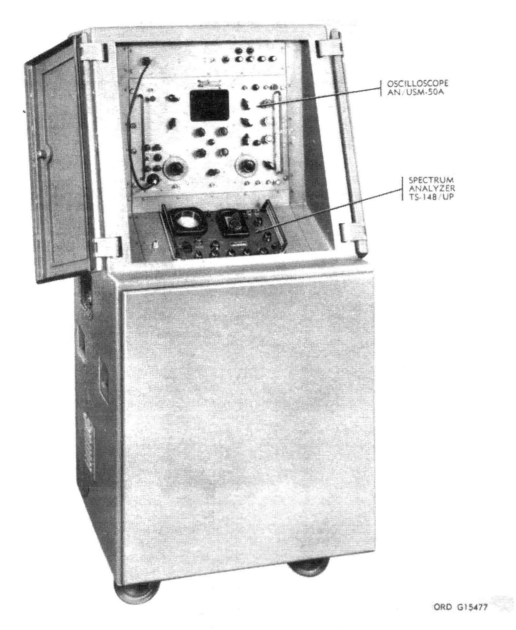

Figure 9. Oscilloscope and spectrum analyzer.

MMS SUBCOURSE NUMBER 151, NIKE MISSILE AND TEST EQUIPMENT
EXERCISES FOR LESSON 4

1. What furnishes external power to the guidance set during checkout?

    A. External power supply-8516630
    B. RF test set-9143471
    C. Electrical test set-9034602
    D. AF and power test set

2. How often does the microsecond oscillator in the RF test set require calibration?

    A. Monthly
    B. Bimonthly
    C. Weekly
    D. Before each use

3. What furnishes filament voltage for the circuits in the upper drawer of the RF and pulse components test set upper drawer?

    A. 300-volt power supply
    B. +240-volt power supply
    C. -60-volt power supply
    D. +150-volt power supply

4. What type of oscillator circuit is used in the microsecond oscillator of the transponder control test set group?

    A. Wein-bridge
    B. Free-running
    C. One-shot multivibrator
    D. Phantastron

5. What is the main purpose for which electrical test set 9005609 is used?

    A. Calibrate missile test equipment
    B. Isolate malfunctions
    C. Confirm accuracy of other test equipment
    D. Measure AC and DC voltage and current

6. Which voltage does the AC power supply in the RF and pulse components test set group upper drawer produce?

    A. 120 volt, 400 Hertz
    B. 120 volts, 1,700 Hertz
    C. 120 volts, 200 Hertz
    D. -28 volts, 1,700 Hertz

7. Which is a mode of operation used by the pulse generator in the lower equipment drawer of the RF and pulse components test set group?

    A. Auto sync
    B. Sync
    C. Monostable
    D. Bistable

8. Which is the attenuation ratio of the AN/USM-50A test probe?

    A. 1:1
    B. 4:1
    C. 5:1
    D. 10:1

9. What produces the positive and negative pitch and yaw pulses in the RF and pulse components test set?

    A. 0.25-microsecond pulse generator
    B. 5-microsecond pulse generator
    C. Variable delay pulse generator
    D. Variable delay and width pulse generator

10. What missile test equipment is used to measure the quality of resonant cavities?

    A. Oscilloscope
    B. Spectrum analyzer
    C. RF test set
    D. Electrical test set

11. Which test point on electrical test set 9005609 is used for a common connection between the source of voltage to be measured and the test set?

    A. TP7
    B. TP4
    C. TP3
    D. TP1

12. What is the maximum input to the AN/USM-50A oscilloscope using the test probe?

    A. 90 volts
    B. 100 volts
    C. 300 volts
    D. 450 volts

13. Which adapter is used for checking the vane axial fans from the flight simulator at the RF and pulse components test set group?

    A. 1201
    B. 1202
    C. 1207
    D. 1211

14. How is the relay assembly in the RF and pulse components test set group activated?

    A. Run-down of the 5-minute timer
    B. Load assembly toggle switch
    C. ON-OFF switch
    D. TEST-POWER switch

15. What part of the transponder control test set is used to determine if the missile guidance set is responding properly to the guidance commands?

    A. Calibrator switch
    B. Power supply
    C. Response meter
    D. Voltage amplifier

16. The start of the time base generated by the gating and switching pulse generator in the transponder control test set group is in coincidence with which coded pulse?

    A. Pulse number 1
    B. Pulse number 2
    C. Pulse number 3
    D. Burst pulse

17. What is used to transfer RF energy from the transponder control test set to the unit under test?

    A. TA 11-3
    B. Antenna coupler
    C. Cable 1410
    D. Waveguide assembly

18. What supplies the timing interval for the generation of the pitch and yaw command in the RF and pulse components test set group?

    A. Coincidence detector
    B. Spectrum analyzer
    C. Electrical test set
    D. RF test set

19. What in the transponder control test set group generates the pitch and yaw command gate?

    A. P and Y pulse generator
    B. Gating and switching pulse generator
    C. Microsecond oscillator
    D. Waveform converter

20. What is the maximum DC voltages, in volts, that can be measured with electrical test set 9005609?

    A. 10
    B. 20
    C. 100
    D. 500

LESSON 5. FIELD MAINTENANCE SHOPS 1, 2, AND 3, AND EMERGENCY CONTACT UNIT

MMS Subcourse No 151	Nike Missile and Test Equipment
Lesson Objective	To give you a general knowledge of the purpose, capabilities, physical description, and basic function of the test consoles comprising shops 1, 2, and 3, to include console layout, types of test modules used during operation of the shops, and maintenance problem areas.
Credit Hours	Four

TEXT

1. **INTRODUCTION.**

   a. **General.** The test equipment used to support the Nike Hercules and improved Nike Hercules battery is identified by two major areas of use. One group is the missile test equipment which is used to test, troubleshoot, and repair the missile and launching equipment. This equipment was covered in lesson 4. The other group which is used to test, troubleshoot, and repair assemblies from equipment in the radar course directing central (RCDC) will be discussed in this lesson. The equipment in both groups is used by direct support, general support, and depot maintenance personnel to keep the Nike batteries in a combat ready status. Efficient use of this test equipment is extremely important in keeping the Nike battery prepared to engage hostile forces.

   b. **Electronic shops 1, 2, and 3.** Part of the support maintenance test equipment, also referred to as field maintenance test equipment, is housed in three van-type trailers designated as electronic shop 1, electronic shop 2, and electronic shop 3. These shops contain console mounted test equipment and accessories. At permanent support or depot maintenance installations, these consoles may be removed from the vans and placed in a shop building to facilitate better work flow and production control. The consoles in each shop are referred to as test positions. Positions 1, 2, and 3 are in shop 1; positions 4 and 5 are in shop 2; and positions 6 and 7 are in shop 3. Test equipment mounted in various panels of each position is classified into three categories as follows:

   (1) Government issue items, such as multimeters and vacuum tube voltmeters.

   (2) Contract purchase items (commercial test equipment), such as signal generators and frequency counters.

   (3) Special engineer design circuits or actual circuits found in the RCDC equipment.

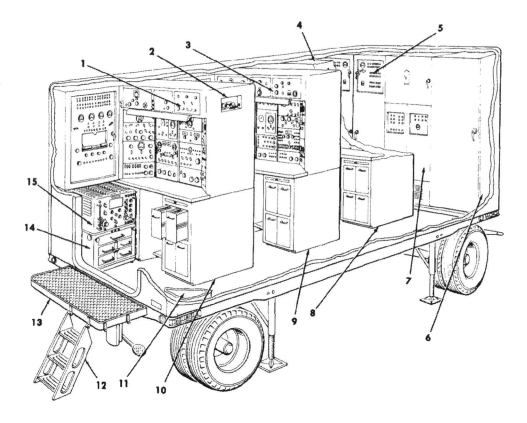

1 Servo test set AN/MPM-48A – position 3
2 Telephone handset
3 Servo test set AN/MPM-47 – position 2
4 Computer test set AN/MPM-45 – position 1
5 Power supply set AN/MSQ-31
6 Storage cabinet
7 Personnel heater
8 Electrical test and maintenance table 1
9 Electrical test and maintenance table 2
10 Electrical test and maintenance table 3
11 Utility cabinet
12 Access ladder
13 Rear platform
14 Oscilloscope dolly
15 Oscilloscope

Figure 1. Electronic shop 1 - cutaway view.

c. **Emergency contact unit.** The other support maintenance test equipment, consisting of unmounted test equipment, is housed in an M109 shop van. This van is referred to as the emergency contact unit (ECU). The ECU is used for on-site testing of HIPAR assemblies which are NOT easily movable to electronic shops 1, 2, and 3. Shop 3 will be covered in a separate paragraph from shops 1 and 2 because shop 3 employs a different scheme of operation.

2. **DESCRIPTION OF SHOP 1 AND SHOP 2.**

a. **General.** The major assemblies of electronic shop 1 (fig 1) are the computer test set AN/MPM-45 (position 1), servo test set AN/MPM-47 (position 2), servo test set AN/MPM-48A (position 3), and the power supply set AN/MSQ-31. The major assemblies of electronic shop 2 (fig 2) are the radar test set AN/MPM-43 (position 4), electrical power test set AN/MPM-42 and radar test set AN/MPM-37A (position 5), and power supply group OS-1065/MPM-34. Each test set is used to test assemblies having common or closely related functions and to determine the quality of operation and acceptability of the assembly. The power supply sets in both shops supply DC voltages, preknock and sync pulses, and distribute AC voltages to the test sets. Each test set is independently operated and contains facilities for controlling the magnitude of input power from the power supply sets.

MMS 151, 5-P2

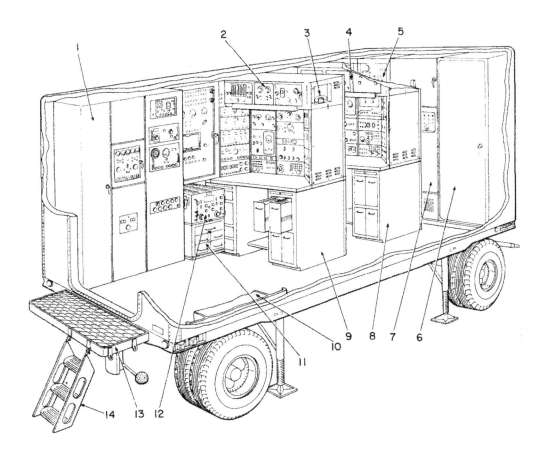

1. Radar test set AN/MPM-37A—position 5
2. Electrical power test set AN/MPM-42—position 5
3. Telephone handset
4. Radar test set AN/MPM-43—position 4
5. Power supply group OA-1065/MPM-34
6. Storage cabinet
7. Personnel heater
8. Electrical test and maintenance table 4
9. Electrical test and maintenance table 5
10. Storage cabinet
11. Oscilloscope dolly
12. Oscilloscope
13. Rear platform
14. Access ladder

Figure 2. Electronic shop 2 - cutaway view.

b. Computer test set AN/MPM-45 (fig 3). Position 1 provides test equipment for testing computer assemblies and for testing voltage regulators, amplifiers, relays, converters, reference generators, brush recorders, and oscillators of the guided missile system radar-signal simulator station AN/MPQ-36. The computer test set, as well as other test sets in shops 1 and 2, is mounted on top of an electrical test and maintenance table. The electrical test and maintenance table at each position contains storage space for manuals, patch cards, miscellaneous test equipment, and cables used at that position. The major difference between each console is the type test equipment mounted in the electrical equipment cabinet panels. This provides capability for testing different units at each console.

c. Servo test set AN/MPM-47 (fig 4). Position 2 contains facilities for testing range, azimuth, and elevation indicators; acquisition and track range amplifier-control groups from the LOPAR and tracking radars; amplifiers, generators, converters, servomotors and the CRT scanners of the AN/MPQ-36 simulator.

MMS 151, 5-P3

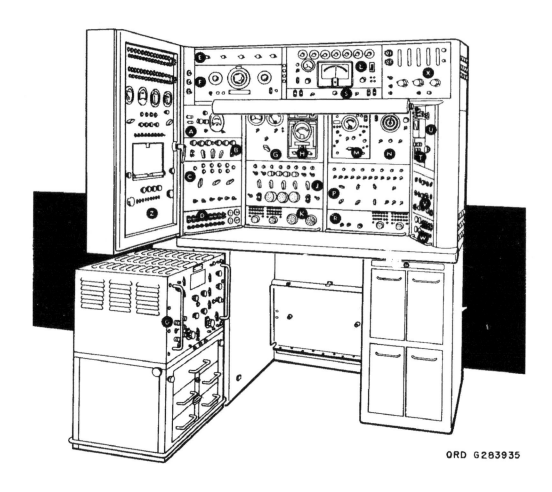

A	Electronic voltmeter	N	Continuity and insulation test set
B	Electrical test panel	O	Oscilloscope
C	Relay test set	P	Electrical test panel
D	Electrical test panel SB–517B/MPM	R	Test connection jack assembly
E	Zero set amplifier test set	S	Test connection generator panel
F	Audio oscillator TS–312/FSM–1	T	Electronic voltmeter
G	Electrical test panel	U	Control panel
H	Multimeter TS–352/U	V	Servo modulator test set
J	Zero set, varistor, and dc amplifier test panel	W	Electrical test panel SB–518B/MPM
K	Test connection jack assembly	X	Electronic counter
L	Resistance bridge	Z	Power distribution panel SB–690/MPM
M	Megohmmeter		

Figure 3. Computer test set AN/MPM-45.

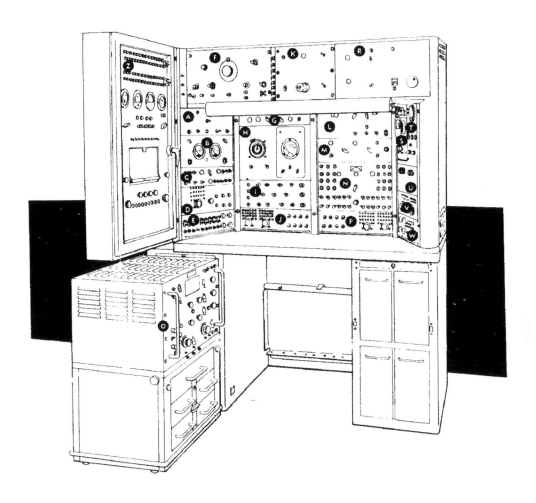

- A Pulse generator
- B Electrical test panel
- C Sweep generator amplifier
- D Jack assembly
- E Electrical test panel
- F Pulse generator
- G Pulse generator
- H Multimeter stop timer
- I Range servo test set
- J Jack assembly
- K Control panel
- L 4-KC signal generator dummy load
- M Electrical test panel
- N Indicator test set
- O Oscilloscope
- P Jack assembly
- R Range calibrator set
- S Electronic voltmeter
- T Indicator high voltage control panel
- U Electrical dummy load
- V Jack assembly
- W Electrical test panel
- Z Power distribution panel

Figure 4. Servo test set AN/MPM-47.

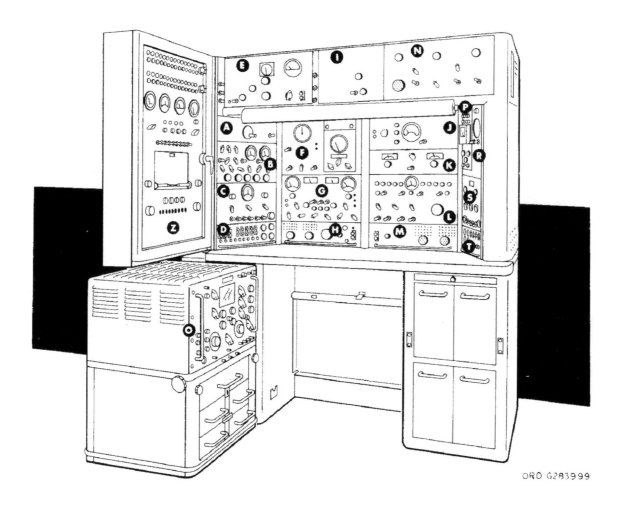

A	Electrical test panel	K	Synchro test set
B	Power distribution panel	L	Servo test set
C	Servo test set	M	Jack assembly
D	Electrical test panel	N	Servo test set group
E	Test set oscillator	O	Oscilloscope LA-239C
F	Multimeter stop timer	P	Electronic voltmeter
G	Servo test control panel	R	Dynamic loudspeaker
H	Jack assembly	S	Servo test set
I	Audio frequency amplifier	T	Electrical test panel
J	AC electronic voltmeter	Z	Power distribution panel

Figure 5. Servo test set AN/MPM-48A.

d. **Servo test set AN/MPM-48A** (fig 5). Position 3 contains facilities for testing servos, amplifiers, and communication assemblies of the Nike Hercules system. Facilities are also provided for testing scoring panels, target coordinate generators, and power supplies.

e. **Radar test set AN/MPM-43** (fig 6). Position 4 provides facilities for testing IF and video amplifiers and components of the command coder set. It also contains facilities for testing units of the guided missile radar-signal simulator stations.

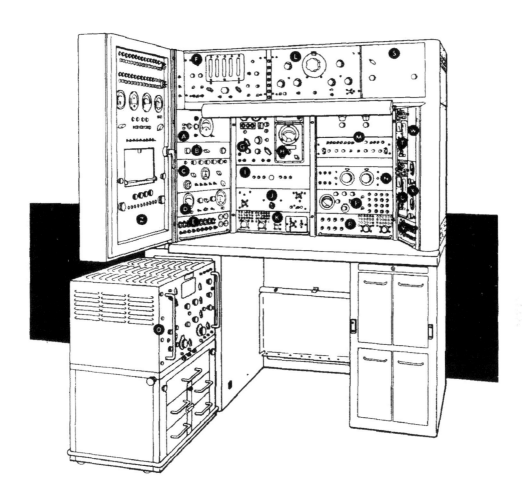

A	Electronic voltmeter	M	Sweep generator
B	Control panel	N	Attenuator
C	Electrical test panel	O	Oscilloscope LA-239C
D	Modulator test set	P	IF components test set
E	Electrical test panel SB–517B/MPM	R	Test connection jack assembly
F	Electronic counter	S	Signal generator assembly
G	Control panel	T	Electronic voltmeter (GR 1800B)
H	Multimeter TS–352/U	U	Electronic voltmeter (GR 1800B)
I	Phase comparison test set	V	Electrical test panel SB–518B/MPM
J	Wide band amplifier	X	Dual differential electronic voltmeter
K	Electrical test panel	Z	Power distribution panel SB–690/MPM
L	Pulse generator (HP 212AR)		

Figure 6. Radar test set AN/MPM-43.

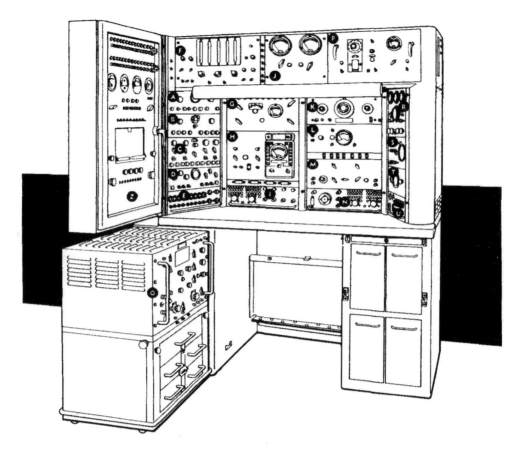

A	Test set subassembly	L	Electronic voltmeter and test connection jack assembly
B	Electrical test panel		
C	Pulse generator	M	RF test set test set
D	Electrical test panel	N	Electrical test panel
E	Electrical test panel SB-517B/MPM	O	Oscilloscope
F	Electronic counter	P	RF test set
G	Control panel test set	R	Power supply test set
H	Multimeter–load and pulse simulator	S	Interval timer test set
I	Test connection jack assembly	T	Control panel
J	RF power meter	U	Electrical test panel SB-518B/MPM
K	Audio oscillator TS-312/FSM-1	Z	Power distribution panel SB-690/MPM

Figure 7. Electrical power test set AN/MPM-42.

f. Electrical power test set AN/MPM-42 (fig 7). The electrical power test set provides facilities for testing low voltage power supplies and regulators, high voltage supplies, delay timers, servos, servomotors, amplifier assemblies, and miscellaneous control panels.

g. Radar test set AN/MPM-37A (fig 8). This part of position 5 is used with the electrical power test set AN/MPM-42 to test Nike track radar high voltage power supplies, modulators, and RF units. It permits testing of a complete RF system, which is too large to bring into the shop, by providing connections through the trailer wall to the RF system located outside.

h. Storage. In addition to the consoles, shops 1 and 2 contain a storage cabinet, a personnel heater, and a utility cabinet (6, 7, and 11, fig 1, respectively for shop 1). Additional storage facilities are provided in each electrical test and maintenance table. The electrical test and maintenance table at each position as well as other storage places use an alphanumeric system of location as shown in figure 9. The vertical bays have alphabetical designations while the horizontal bays have numerical designations. There is also storage space in the rear of each electrical test and maintenance table. Each position is layed out in the same manner to facilitate rapid location of any test equipment or accessory needed by

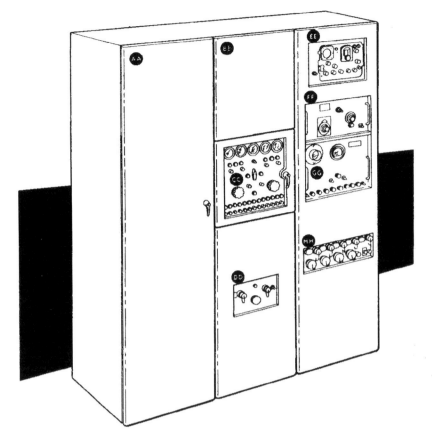

AA Trigger amplifier AM–1104A/M
Radar modulator MD–243A/M
Power supply PP–1191/M
Power supply PP–1162/MS
BB Trigger amplifier AM–1104A/M
Radar modulator MD–243A/M
CC Control panel
DD Electrical dummy load
EE Spectrum analyzer TS–148/UP
FF Spectrum analyzer
GG Spectrum analyzer
HH Test connection jack assembly
JJ[1] Test connection jack assembly

[1] This assembly is not illustrated. It is located on the rear of radar test set AN/MPM–37 and protrudes through the outside wall of electronic shop van trailer XM383.

Figure 8. Radar test set AN/MPM-37A.

the technician to perform a particular test.

i. **Miscellaneous test equipment.**

(1) *General.* The miscellaneous test equipment used in shops 1 and 2 consists of unmounted test equipment; cables and test lead sets 1, 2, 3, 4, and 5; adapters and fixture sets 1, 2, 3, 4, and 5; and electrical contact assembly sets 1, 2, 3, 4, and 5. Shop 1 and shop 2 miscellaneous test equipment is discussed in (2) through (5) below.

(2) *Unmounted test equipment* (fig 10). The unmounted test equipment supplements the

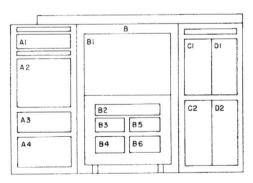

Figure 9. Electrical test and maintenance table and oscilloscopy dolly - typical for position 1, 2, 3, 4, and 5.

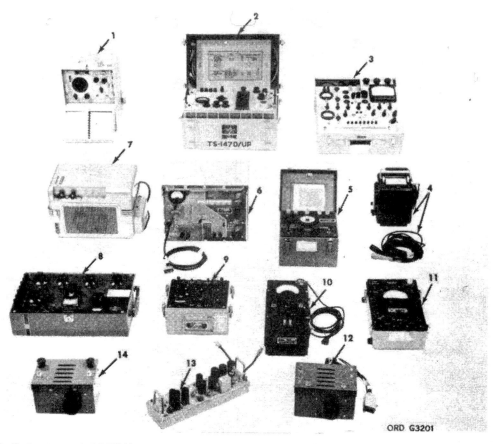

1 Frequency meter TS-323/UR
2 Radar test set TS-147D/UP
3 Tube tester
4 Insulation resistance tester ZM-21A/U and cable
5 Frequency-power meter ME-51/UP
6 Analyzer ZM-3/U
7 Test recorder
8 Null voltage test set
9 Resistance bridge ZM-4B/U
10 Electronic multimeter ME-6/U
11 Multimeter TS-352/U
12 Pulse generator
13 Receiver control
14 Receiver-gate generator

Figure 10. Unmounted test equipment.

mounted test equipment in performing tests on assemblies. The pulse generator and receiver-gate generator (12 and 14, fig 10) are stored in storage location A2 of the electrical test and maintenance table at position 1. The electronic multimeter and multimeter TS-352/U (10 and 11, fig 10) are stored in rear of the electrical test and maintenance table 1 at storage location A1. The remaining unmounted test equipment in figure 10 is stored in the storage cabinet (6, fig 1).

(3) Cables and test leads sets 1, 2, 3, 4, and 5. Table I gives you an example of how the cables are listed in technical manuals. This table is typical and reflects information found in technical manuals stored in the electrical test and maintenance tables of shops 1 and 2. It shows the part number of each cable and, by reference to illustrations, shows the storage location of each cable. The 100-, 200-, 300-, 400-, and 500-series

TABLE I. CABLES

ITEM	PART NO	STORAGE LOCATION REFERENCE
Cable 101	8157650	2 in A1, 2 in B1, rear of 9, fig 1
Cable 102	8157651	C1, rear of 9, fig 1
Cable 103	8150933	D1, rear of 9, fig 1
Cable 104	8150934	D1, rear of 9, fig 1
Cable 201	8151081	A1 and B1, rear of 9, fig 1
Cable 202	8151082	C1, rear of 10, fig 1
Cable 235	9140631	A4, 9, fig 1
Cable 301	8151221	2 in B1, 11, fig 1
Cable 302	8151222	B1, 11, fig 1
Cable 303	8151223	B1, 11, fig 1

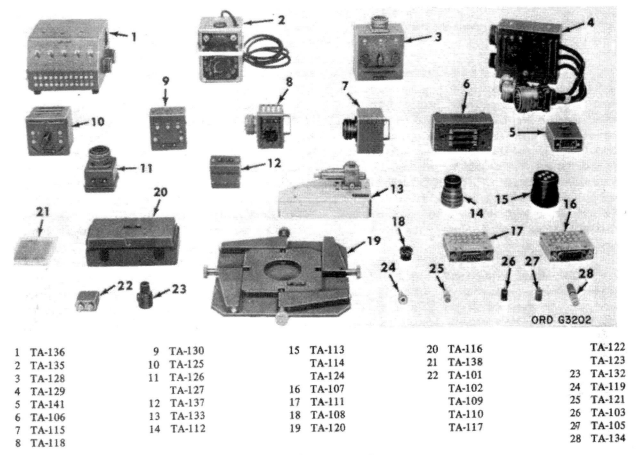

1	TA-136	9	TA-130	15	TA-113	20	TA-116		TA-122
2	TA-135	10	TA-125		TA-114	21	TA-138		TA-123
3	TA-128	11	TA-126		TA-124	22	TA-101	23	TA-132
4	TA-129		TA-127	16	TA-107		TA-102	24	TA-119
5	TA-141	12	TA-137	17	TA-111		TA-109	25	TA-121
6	TA-106	13	TA-133	18	TA-108		TA-110	26	TA-103
7	TA-115	14	TA-112	19	TA-120		TA-117	27	TA-105
8	TA-118							28	TA-134

Figure 11. 100-series test adapters.

cables are used in various combinations to perform tests at positions 1, 2, 3, 4, and 5, respectively. It can be seen from the accompanying table that each cable is stored in a location which makes it easily accessible to the technician working at the individual consoles.

(4) Adapters and fixtures sets 1, 2, 3, 4, and 5. An example of the test adapters used to perform tests in electronic shop 1 is given in table II. The part number for each item and a reference to illustrations showing physical appearance and storage location of each item are included in the table. The 100-, 200-, and 300-series test adapters are used in various combinations to perform tests at positions 1, 2, and 3, respectively. The 400- and 500-series test adapters are used in shop 2, at positions 4 and 5, respectively. The functional use of each item is given in the description column of the table. The 100-series test adapters are shown in figure 11. The only improved Nike-Hercules test adapter appearing in the 100-series components is TA-C139 and is indicated by the INH suffix. The 200-, 300-, 400-, and 500-series components are not shown but are stored in a location easily accessible to the technician working at the respective consoles.

TABLE II. TEST ADAPTERS

ITEM	PART NO	FIG REF PHYSICAL APPEARANCE	STORAGE LOCATION	DESCRIPTION
TA-101	8156115	22, fig 7	E7, rear of 9, fig 1	2.2-megohm standard resistor adapter
TA-102	8156116	22, fig 7	E7, rear of 9, fig 1	10-megohm standard resistor adapter
TA-103	8157653	26, fig 7	2 in E7, rear of 9, fig 1	Tip jack adapter
TA-C139 (INH)	9980829	(not shown)	F8, rear of 9, fig 1	Adapter

j. **Electrical contact assembly sets 1, 2, 3, 4, and 5.**

(1) The electrical contact assembly sets 1, 2, and 3 (patch cards) of electronic shop 1 are used at positions 1, 2, and 3, respectively. Sets 4 and 5 of electronic shop 2 are used at positions 4 and 5, respectively. Patch cards for position 1 are stored in drawers C1, C2, D1, and D2 (fig 1) of electrical test and maintenance table 1. Patch cards for positions 2, 3, 4, and 5 are stored in drawers C1, D1, and D2 of electrical test and maintenance tables 2, 3, 4, and 5, respectively. Each patch card is applicable to a particular test as specified in technical bulletins covering the test being performed.

(2) A patch card consists of three phenolic blocks mounted on a common metallic frame. Metallic contact studs are mounted in perforations on the phenolic block. The contact studs are cross-connected as required on the rear of the patch card. When the patch card is placed in the patching panel (located on panel Z at each position), the door of the patching panel is closed and patch card contact studs make contact with similar studs on the patching panel. This establishes connections only for those circuits of the test set required for testing a particular assembly. Patch cards are slotted on each side to prevent incorrect insertion. Each patching panel contains a lever operated interlock switch which, when closed, provides ground to relays so that the test set can be energized to ON, provided a patch card is inserted and the door interlocks are closed.

3. OPERATION AND USE OF SHOPS 1 AND 2.

a. **General.** When a chassis, assembly, or subassembly (referred to as units under test (UUT)), arrives at a Nike direct or general support unit, it has a DA Form 2407 (maintenance request) attached to it. The job order clerk assigns the chassis a control number to identify it with the 2407. The chassis is passed on to an inspection section where it is given a visual inspection to determine if any components are missing or broken, then an inspection tag is attached to the chassis. The position used to test the chassis is determined from a master technical bulletin and the chassis is sent to the appropriate shop position for testing and repair.

b. **Master technical bulletin.** Master TB 9-4900-250-35/1 is used to determine which position of shop 1, 2, or 3 is used to test the UUT. TB 9-4900-250-35/2 is used to determine which missile and launcher test equipment is used to test UUT's or assemblies from the launching area. Table III gives you an example of the information found in master TB 9-4900-250-35/1. In this table the UUT's are indexed by part number sequence. The part number stamped on the chassis to be tested will identify the UUT, and the position column of table III identifies the console used to test the UUT. The TM or TB number column identifies the manual or bulletin to be used when performing the test. The chapter column identifies the chapter of the TM or TB which concerns the particular UUT. The date and latest change number of the TM or TB is also given in the master TB.

c. **Use of technical manuals.** At the appropriate position the correct TM or TB is selected for testing the UUT. Each chapter in the TM or TB contains the following information.

(1) Purpose of the test. This section explains what the test checks.

(2) Test equipment. This section lists the panels of the console, miscellaneous test equipment, cables, adapters, and patch cards which the technician will need to perform the test. From this information all the test equipment and accessories can be selected from their storage locations.

(3) Preparation for test. This section contains information on how to condition the console for making the test and how to connect the UUT to the console. It also tells which patch card to insert in the patching panel. From this information the technician

TABLE III. MASTER TECHNICAL BULLETIN

PART NO	SPEC NO	POSITION	TM OR TB NO	CHAP	DATE	CHANGE NO
9140712	GS-58611	2	TM 9-1400-250-34/2/2	21	16 Sep 64	C1
9140745	GS-57536	2	TM 9-1400-250-35/2/3	4	15 Sep 64	
9140754	GS-56957	5	TM 9-1400-250-34/5/4	5	28 Oct 64	
9140767	GS-18353	3	TM 9-1400-250-34/3/2	9	28 Apr 64	

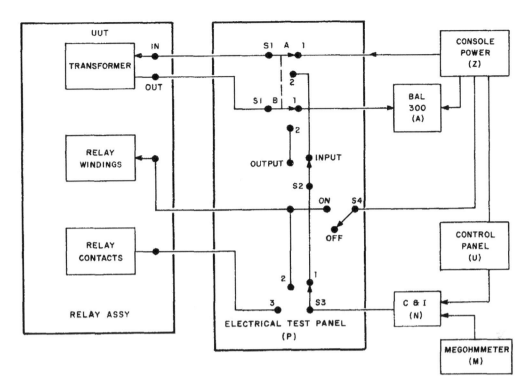

Figure 12. Typical test layout.

sets switches, potentiometers, and other controls to the designated position and connects the UUT to the correct console panels. The technician then places the correct patch card in the patching panel and closes the door to the patching panel.

(4) *Acceptance test.* This section gives a step by step procedure for testing the UUT. Signals, biases, and other voltages which the UUT receives from the console are adjusted by the technician to those values which the UUT is supposed to receive when it is a component in the Nike Hercules or improved Hercules system. In addition to describing these voltages, this section contains pictures of waveshapes to be observed and adjustments to be made on the UUT. Any time the UUT fails to comply with the normal indications listed in this section, the step numbers it failed are recorded on the inspection tag attached to the UUT. The step number of the acceptance test which the UUT failed will localize the problem. When all the steps of this test are performed and the actual indications are the same as those described in this section, the UUT passes.

(5) *Maintenance.* This section gives a detailed schematic and verbal analysis of how the UUT is supposed to function. It also contains a test layout that shows connections between the UUT and console. By using the step number failed, detail schematic of the UUT, and verbal description of how the UUT is supposed to function, the technician proceeds to locate the faulty component. When located, the faulty component is replaced and the acceptance test is continued until it is completed. When the UUT passes the acceptance test, it is returned to supply channels or to the Nike battery. A block diagram for a typical test layout and the test performed at position 1 is illustrated in figure 12. The panels on shop 1 used for this particular test are A, M, N, P, U, and Z. The test and checks are performed through electrical test panel (P) by switching in the following manner:

(a) *Voltage check.* When S1-A and S1-B (which are ganged together) are in position 1, S1-A supplies power from the console to the transformer in the UUT and S1-B connects the output of the transformer to the BAL 300 (electronic voltmeter) on panel A of the console for an output voltage reading.

(b) *Continuity and insulation check.* This check is performed by placing S3 to position 1 and S2 to the input position (as shown in fig 12). Continuity of the transformer input winding is then checked by

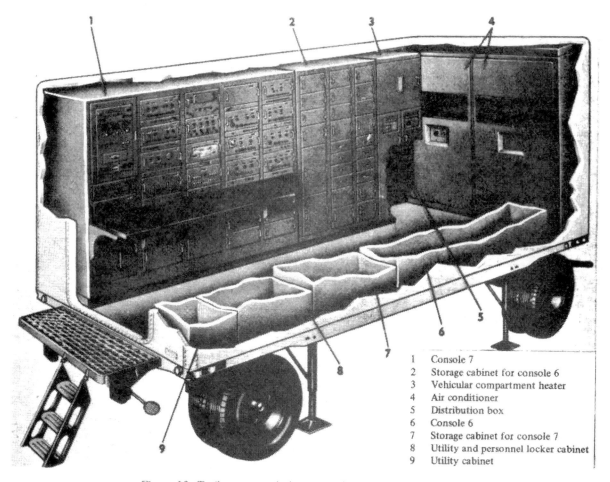

1 Console 7
2 Storage cabinet for console 6
3 Vehicular compartment heater
4 Air conditioner
5 Distribution box
6 Console 6
7 Storage cabinet for console 7
8 Utility and personnel locker cabinet
9 Utility cabinet

Figure 13. Trailer mounted electronic shop 3 - cutaway view.

placing S1-A and B to position 2 and reading the resistance on panel (M). Continuity and insulation of the transformer output winding is checked by placing S2 to the output position and reading the resistance on panel (M). Connection of panel (M) and (N) are controlled at panel (N).

(c) Relay check. Continuity of the relay windings is checked by placing S3 to position 2 and reading the resistance on panel (M). The open circuit resistance of the relay contacts is checked by placing S3 to position 3. Both positions of S3 connect the relay to panel (N). When S3 is in position 3, S4 can be placed ON to energize the relay and the closed circuit resistance of the relay contacts is read on panel (M).

4. **DESCRIPTION OF SHOP 3.**

a. **General.** The addition of shop 3 (fig 13) to the Nike field maintenance test equipment (FMTE) was necessary when TTR, HIPAR, and AN/MPQ-T1 were added to the basic Nike Hercules system. The conversion of a Nike Hercules FMTE system to an improved Nike Hercules FMTE system consisted of adding electronic shop 3 to the basic system and modifying electronic shops 1 and 2. The modifications to these electronic shops consisted of equalizing the workload on some of the consoles by transferring certain units under test from these consoles to the new electronic shop 3. In addition, some of the improved Nike Hercules system chassis are checked in electronic shops 1 and 2, but most of these units were assigned to consoles which had light workloads. Shops 1 and 2 had to be modified to receive the newly assigned UUT's. The modifications consisted primarily of removing the technical bulletins, test adapters, and patch cards of the units under test which were transferred to electronic shop 3. At the same time new technical bulletins, patch cards, and test adapters were added for the newly assigned UUT. One hundred and ninety-five units have been assigned to electronic shop 3. Eighteen of the 195 units are Nike Ajax/Hercules units which reduced the traffic on consoles in electronic shops 1 and 2. Twenty-five improved Nike Hercules units, excluding HIPAR, were assigned to consoles 1, 2, 3, and 5 in electronic shops 1 and 2. These units are modified units of the basic Nike Ajax/Hercules systems and therefore may be checked on these consoles without any wiring changes being made in the consoles. The 18 units transferred to electronic shop 3 consist primarily of large turnover units such as IF amplifiers, AFC units, synchronizers, and IF-to-video detectors. This assignment is tentative and subject to change as a result of system changes. The layout of the equipment in electronic shop 3 is shown in figure 13. Two separate and independent test consoles with associated storage cabinets are provided. The test consoles are basically identical; the storage cabinets are similar, varying only in storage details. The two consoles are designated consoles 6 and 7. Console 6 is located on the curbside of the trailer while console 7 is located on the roadside of the trailer. The test consoles and storage cabinets are designed to permit ready installation at permanent locations. Each console in electronic shop 3 contains a limited number of test equipment panels which allows it to test a specific category of units. As test requirements change, dictating a different or modified test equipment lineup or perhaps even a complete change in the testing capability of an individual console, these plug-in test equipment panels may be replaced by a different group of panels. The unused panels may then be mounted in the storage cabinets which are specifically designed to accept them. This capability of ready console conversion, coupled with the facility of storage of alternate test equipment panels, provides the flexibility necessary for modifications.

    b.   **Console 6.**

NOTE: Information in (1), (2), (3), (4), and (7) below applies to console 7 (fig 15) as well as console 6.

    (1) *General.* Console 6 (fig 14) in electronic shop 3 is composed of rectangular modules, 7 inches high by 19 inches wide. The modules are mounted in five bays, 60 inches high by 19 inches wide. The vertical bays are designated A through E (left to right facing the console). In the individual bays, each slot is assigned a number beginning with 1 at the top and proceeding downward. This also applies to the small cable connection areas, or reentry strips, which occupy space between modules. The identification (for the purpose of locating any exposed console area) is given by a letter followed by a number. This identification is placed on the console frame to the right side of the space and any module placed within that space assumes the designated area identification. For example, the third area from the top in the third bay from the left is called C3. When the console operator is instructed to perform some type of operation at panel C3, he will be able to find that location immediately by observing the front of the console. The associated ordnance number is also displayed on the front panel of each module. A small removable plate bearing the ordnance number is mounted on the upper right-hand portion of the module. When the ordnance number is caused to change, the plate mounting is loosened behind the panel, and the plate is replaced with one bearing the new ordnance number.

    (2) *Location of the connected UUT and test accessories.* The connectors for the interconnection of the UUT and the console are located just above the workbench on the electrical test panel located in area A4. The operator is normally positioned in front of area C with the UUT in front of area B7. This position leaves the work surface directly in front and to the right free for use by the operator. The test consoles are so arranged that the outer bays and center bays below the work surface contain those items of test equipment seldom used. The center three bays above the work surface contain those items normally used by the operator. Thus the operator has within easy reach and ready vision all the equipment normally used during a test procedure.

    (3) *Location of the patch panel.* The electrical power distribution panel is located in area A1 (fig 14) and contains the circuitry for energizing the console. No attempt was made toward programming the operation of this panel. This unit also contains the test connection patching panel which is in area A3. The patching panel is the same multicontact switch assembly used on shop 1 and 2 consoles. The insertion of the individual prewired patch card associated with each unit under test provides the proper interconnections of the UUT to the test console. The patching switch is used in electronic shop 3 because it is still the most reliable and economical device available for accomplishing a large scale switching operation. The remaining units within the consoles of electronic shop 3 may be divided into four functional groups: the console programming equipment, display and measuring equipment, special purpose test equipment and power supplies. The location of these units is discussed in (4) through (7) below.

    (4) *Location of the console programming equipment (CPE).* A card reader and an associated remote switching control, which comprise the console

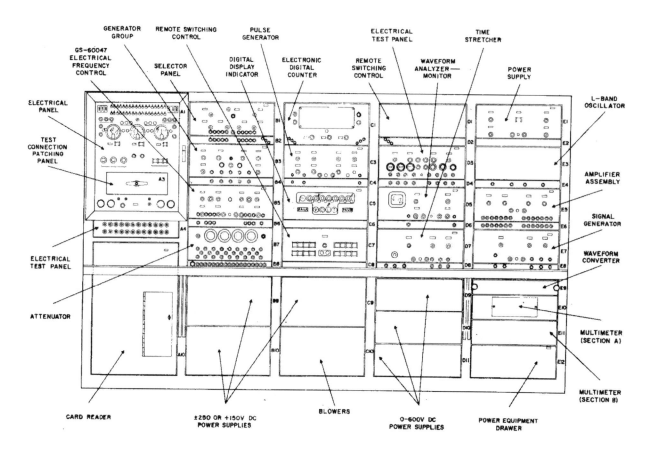

Figure 14. Console 6 - location diagram.

programming equipment, are located in areas A10 and C7, respectively. The card reader may be pulled forward on drawer slides to facilitate maintenance procedures. The remote switching control is centrally located within the console where it is easily accessible to the console operator.

(5) Location of the display and measuring equipment (DAME). The units within the display and measuring equipment are located in various places in the consoles. The digital display indicator, the waveform analyzer monitor, and the time stretcher are centrally located within the console in areas C5, D5, and D7, respectively. Thus the console operator has within easy reach and ready vision all the test and monitoring equipment normally needed during any test procedure. An electronic digital counter is located in area C1 and a multimeter, consisting of three sections, is located in areas E9 through E11 of the console. The outputs of the electronic digital counter and the multimeter are displayed on the digital display indicator; therefore, these units do not have to be centrally located.

(6) Location of the special purpose test equipment (SPTE). The special purpose test equipment is located in areas B1 through B8, C3, D1, D3, and E1 through E8. These panels are specifically designed to test a particular category of units. For console 6 these units are designed to check IF amplifiers, AFC units, and video detectors. The panels have been standardized in layout, dimension, connectors, and mounting facilities. As additional special test equipment items are required for checking units of the improved Nike Hercules, they may be readily interchanged with those initially provided. They may be stored in the storage cabinets when not in use and, as required, interchanged with units in the console. The small connector panels or reentry strips between the large panels facilitate interconnecting coaxial type signal leads to the signal switching system. These panels also provide direct access to input and output signals which may be required during maintenance and repair operations on a faulty UUT.

(7) Location of power supplies. The DC

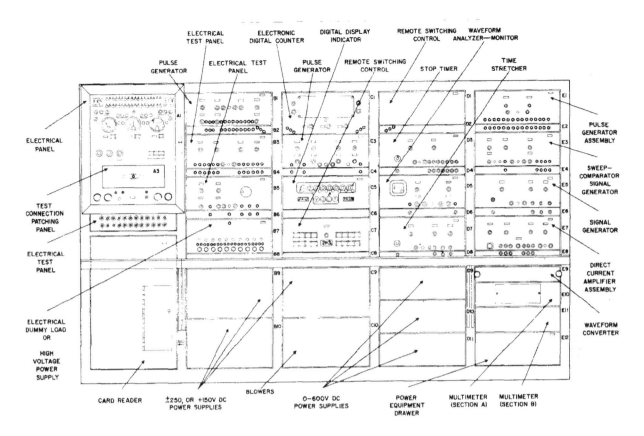

Figure 15. Console 7 - location diagram.

power supplies and voltage regulators are located in areas B9, B10, C9, D9 through D11, and E12. The power supplies are located below the workbench and are not accessible to the operator for maintenance purposes. Also below the workbench and located in area C10 are the blowers which provide cooling and ventilation of the units within the console.

c. **Console 7.**

(1) As depicted in figure 15, the console programming equipment, the display and measuring equipment, and the power supply areas are identical on consoles 6 and 7. The difference in console panels occurs in the special purpose test equipment areas of the B bay, E bay, and areas D1 and D2. These special test equipment panels are used to check video amplifiers, DC amplifiers, pulse generators, relay assemblies, and power supplies. The overall operation of console 7 is identical to the operation of console 6 except for the special purpose test equipment.

(2) All of the panels within the test consoles of electronic shop 3 are constructed to utilize a new concept in the layout of equipment. Each major panel has one or more subassemblies called minispecs. A minispec is a module which contains usually one complete circuit such as an IF amplifier, a pulse generator, or a DC amplifier. A minispec subassembly is 1-1/2 inches wide by 8-1/2 inches long by 3-1/2 inches high. Up to five tube stages may be mounted on this subassembly depending on the complexity of the circuit. In special circuits a double minispec, which is twice the width of a single minispec, is used in order to get a complex circuit on a subassembly. All the minispecs within a panel may function together to produce an output signal, as in the pulse generator, or they may perform separate and independent functions as in the amplifier assembly. The individual minispec contains numerous test points making it possible to check nearly every point within the circuit. For troubleshooting purposes, the minispec is raised from the surrounding units and locked in this position for easier accessibility. The minispec is less difficult to replace than a subassembly of a panel, thus making maintenance and repair easier.

5. **FUNCTION OF SHOP 3 CONSOLES** (FIG 16).

a. **General.** In order to simplify test procedures

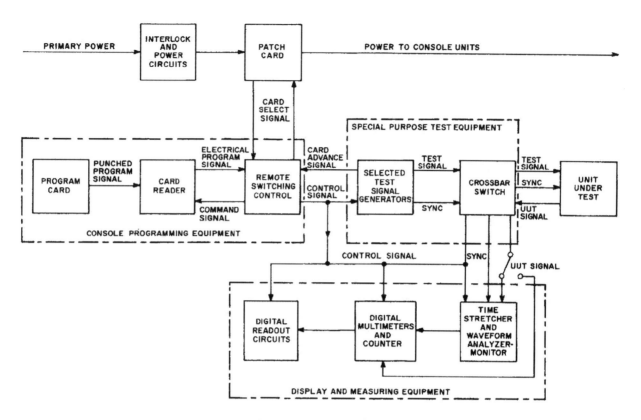

Figure 16. Electronic shop 3 - block diagram.

and have a maximum testing rate of UUT's on a pass-fail basis, a certain degree of automatic console operation is desired. The automation of the setup controls and subsequent positioning or repositioning of controls during the control of a test procedure provides the greatest return in terms of test time saved at a reasonable cost and equipment complexity. With these features in mind, the consoles in electronic shop 3 have been designed to operate semiautomatically. However, facilities are provided for the consoles to be completely manually operated by the console operator for manual repair and maintenance of defective units. The test consoles contain test equipment panels including a number of selector switches that provide the proper output signals and adjust the output measuring equipment to the proper range and characteristics. These switches are rotary type with an actuating solenoid positioning device to position each switch. The console programming equipment functions to position these rotary selector switches to the proper positions in the correct sequence. In addition, the selector switches may be manually operated if required. The functional units within the consoles of electronic shop 3, i.e., the interlocks and power circuits, the console programming equipment, the special purpose test equipment, and the display and measuring equipment, are discussed in paragraphs b thru e below.

b. Interlock and power circuits. These circuits (fig 16) provide the necessary protection and power for operating the console. The patch card for each UUT provides the power interconnections to program the three variable power supplies (0 to 600 volts) and to verify selection of the correct program card. The patch card establishes continuity with verification circuits in the remote switching control. The verification circuit determines that the correct program card for performing test on the UUT is selected by the card reader.

c. Console programming equipment.

(1) To accomplish its required function, the console programming equipment has the capability of addressing a particular panel and positioning a selected switch to any one of a number of discrete positions. The console programming equipment then proceeds to position additional switches in the same panel or other panels in the proper sequence until a complete test procedure has been accomplished. To make effective use of the console programming

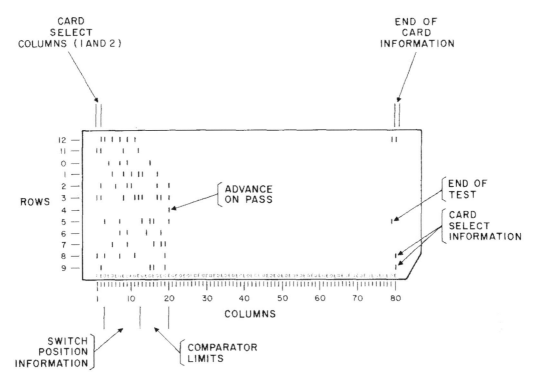

Figure 17. Standard program card.

equipment, as many test equipment controls as possible must be operable in discrete increments. As shown in figure 16, the console programming equipment consists of a program card, card reader, and a remote switching control panel.

(2) All test condition information for semiautomatic console operation is placed on the program card (fig 17) by holes punched in the card. This card is a standard punched card, 3-1/4 by 7-3/8 inches, containing 12 rows and 80 columns. The four classes of information contained on this card are: card select, switch position, comparator limit, and end of card. The card select information is always punched in columns 1 and 2 and is used to find the correct card for a particular UUT. The switch position information is punched in columns 3 and 4. This information is used to select a particular panel, switch, and switch position for the test to be performed. The next eight columns are used to program the comparator limit information which establishes the upper and lower limits of the parameter to be tested. Programming of the switches and the limits completes one test condition. As many test conditions as necessary to check the UUT may be programmed in the same manner. The final information punched on a card is the end of card information. This information is punched either in the last two columns of the card, columns 79 and 80, or at the end of a particular test if the test ends before all columns of the card are used. If all test conditions have been completed, the end of card punches will provide an end of test signal which will be displayed by a front panel indicator on the remote switching control. If another card is required to complete the test, the end of card punches will contain card select information which is used to select the next card required to continue the test.

(3) The program cards are stored in the hopper of the card reader (fig 18). Single cards are automatically picked from the bottom of the deck with a picker knife and pushed into feed rollers. Four sets of clutched rollers transfer cards up the chute to the rotating drum. The card is clamped onto the drum and rotated to the read station. At the read station 12 star wheels are in a position to drop into the holes in the card. Microswitches on the star wheel arms generate program signals when the wheel drops into the punched holes. After the card is read it is rotated to the follow read station and dropped back into the hopper. The program signals from the card reader (fig 16) are applied to the remote switching control which contains logic relay circuits to convert all signals from the card reader into commands to be applied to the desired panel within the console. It is the remote switching control which

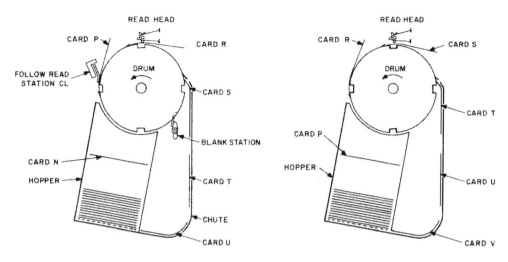

Figure 18. Card reader.

actually addresses the selected console panel, selects a particular switch on the selected panel, and then rotates it to the correct position. Control signals are applied between the remote switching control and nearly every panel within the console. In order for the card reader to select the correct series of program cards for a particular test, card select signals are coupled between the remote switching control and the patch card. The card reader searches for the first program card until the output signals from the card reader energizes a particular combination of logic relays whose contacts complete a patch through the patch card and energizes a card selected relay in the remote switching control. When the first program card of a test series has been selected, a CARD SELECTED visual indication is given to the console operator indicating that the check of the UUT may progress.

d. **Special purpose test equipment.** This special purpose test equipment consists of specifically designed panels which test a particular category of units such as IF amplifiers, AFC units, pulse generators, and DC control units. It is these special test equipment panels which make the two consoles in electronic shop 3 differ. The console programming equipment addresses the panels required for checking the UUT and establishes the proper test signal output which is to be applied to the UUT. The special purpose test equipment consists of synchronizer units, IF and RF signal generators, pulse generators, DC amplifiers, and associated control circuits. The special purpose test equipment has been broadly designed so that it is capable of generating all signals for the improved Nike Hercules system including TRR, HIPAR, and the AN/MPQ-T1 simulator, as well as providing a margin for future growth as required when the improved Nike system is modified. Test signals between the UUT and the special purpose test equipment are applied through a crossbar switch. The crossbar switch is positioned by signals from the remote switching control to set up a path for signals between the UUT and the console equipment. The crossbar switch permits establishment of alternate signal paths, which are required for different test conditions and it also eliminates external cabling between the UUT and the console test panels.

e. **Display and measuring equipment.**

(1) General. The signals from the UUT are applied through the crossbar switch to the display and measuring equipment (DAME). The DAME system consists of a timer stretcher, a waveform analyzer-monitor, a digital counter, a digital multimeter, and a digital readout circuit.

(2) Time stretcher and waveform analyzer-monitor. The time stretcher and waveform analyzer-monitor are used to interpret pulsed signal information. These two units permit pulse characteristics such as pulse duration, amplitude, rise time, and fall time to be measured. The time stretcher converts the pulsed signals to an increased time base so that accurate measurements of the pulse characteristics may be made. For example, a 1-microsecond pulse can be stretched to a pulse duration of 1 second, an increase of one million in time base. The waveform analyzer-monitor actually performs the measurement of the pulse characteristics and applies the measured information to either the digital multimeter or

counter, depending on the characteristics being measured. The time stretcher and waveform analyzer-monitor have the advantage of greater frequency coverage, programmable operation, and simple pushbutton control when manually operated. In addition, the numerical readout of measured parameters requires no interpretation of the results on the part of the operator. These panels provide equipment which requires a minimum of decisionmaking on the part of the operator.

(3) *Digital multimeter and digital counter.* The digital multimeter and the digital counter are the only two measuring instruments within the consoles of electronic shop 3. These instruments are controlled by the console programming equipment in the semiautomatic mode of console operation but they may be manually controlled if necessary. The signal inputs to these measuring units are from the waveform analyzer-monitor when pulsed signals are being measured or from the crossbar switch and sometimes the patch card if continuous wave signals such as AC voltages, DC voltages, resistances, or ratios are being measured. The digital multimeter and digital counter are commercial instruments modified for application in this system. The output from the digital multimeter or digital counter, depending on the measurement being made, is applied to the digital readout circuits.

(4) *Digital readout circuits.* The digital readout circuits display, in numerical form, all the measured quantities of both the test console and the UUT, as shown in figures 14 and 15. In addition to the numerical value of the measured quantity, the characteristic of this quantity is displayed such as volts, ohms, microseconds, etc. The numerical readout value of the signal from the UUT is also compared in these circuits with limits from the console programming equipment which are established by punches in the program card. A visual PASS or FAIL signal is given to the console operator depending on whether or not the signal from the UUT is within programmed limits. A PASS signal permits the semiautomatic console operation to continue, but a FAIL signal or the absence of a PASS signal stops the console programming equipment. If a FAIL condition occurs, the operator can perform troubleshooting procedures while observing the digital readout display. Once the trouble is cleared and a PASS signal is obtained the operator may then place the console programming equipment back into semiautomatic operation.

6. **OPERATION AND USE OF SHOP 3.** The general pattern of testing UUT's in shop 3 is similar to shops 1 and 2. However, since switch positions and most cable connections are made automatically, the operator's main function is to connect the UUT to the console, press buttons, and observe indications on the readout equipment as instructed by technical manuals. The technical manuals covering the UUT's tested in shop 3 are selected by using the master technical bulletin and they contain the same type data as shop 1 and 2 technical manuals; i.e., purpose of test, preparation for test, acceptance test, and troubleshooting aids. The purpose of the test and preparation for test are the same as shops 1 and 2, while the acceptance test gives the number of each test condition, refers to a location by area number, and gives the operation to be performed or observations to be made in that area. The acceptance test also gives the purpose of the test condition. While the acceptance test is being performed, the test equipment is in semiautomatic operation. If the UUT fails the acceptance test, the repairman performs the troubleshooting aids listed in the TM. While performing the troubleshooting aids the test equipment is operated manually. Data given in the troubleshooting aids allow the operator to set each switch and control. If the switches on the console are in the position prescribed by the TM, the trouble is in the UUT. If not, the trouble is in the console.

7. **EMERGENCY CONTACT UNIT** (FIG 19). The support maintenance test equipment used to test some HIPAR assemblies is housed in the emergency contact unit (ECU). This test equipment is normally used by maintenance contact teams which are dispatched from a direct support maintenance shop to the Nike site. The men dispatched with the ECU should be well qualified technicians holding a 23U MOS. The ECU contains test equipment necessary to analyze and evaluate the HIPAR system performance. Many of the test equipment items stored in the ECU are of the commercial type including a differential voltmeter, a tube tester, an oscilloscope, a vacuum tube voltmeter, and a multimeter. Many other ECU test equipment items are made especially for the HIPAR, such as the precision slotted waveguide, a slide screw tuner, a slotted line probe, and a coaxial waveguide adapter.

8. **CALIBRATION.** Most items of test and measuring equipment in shops 1, 2, 3, and the ECU require calibration every 90 days. However, some of this equipment requires calibration at 180-day intervals. Many of the items of test equipment can be calibrated only by authorized calibration teams while other items can be maintenance calibrated by direct support, general support, or depot maintenance personnel. Information on calibration requirements for test equipment in the improved Nike Hercules system as well as other items of

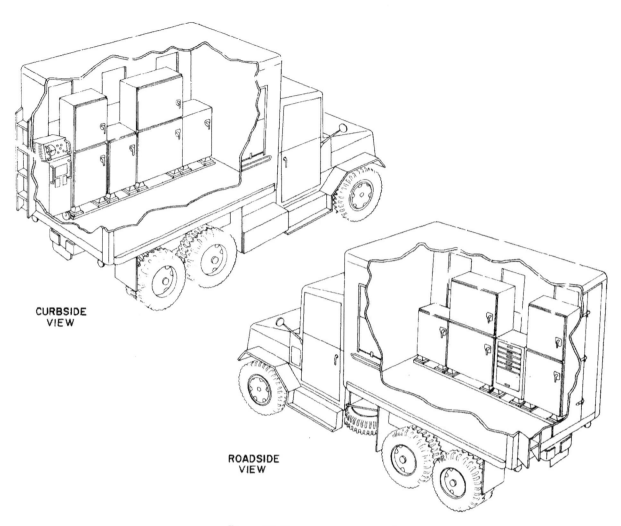

Figure 19. Emergency contact unit.

Army materiel can be found in TB 750-236.

9. MAINTENANCE. The Army's philosophy of constant equipment improvement insures excellent return for the money spent on missile systems in terms of missile effectiveness. As the Nike system is modified, the field maintenance test equipment must also be modified to accommodate these system changes. As the modifications are made to the test equipment, check procedures will change requiring changes to be posted in the technical manuals. If the modifications and changes to TM's are kept current, the shops will retain their capability as effective support maintenance equipment. The Nike system has been deployed sufficiently long for most basic maintenance problems to be solved. However, the card reader in shop 3 is an area where some difficulty exists. The cards tend to "swell" if stored where the humidity is excessively high. Most of the card reader problems are solved by "keeping your cards dry" and by having a well trained operator who keeps the card reader in proper adjustment.

10. SUMMARY. This lesson has presented field maintenance shops 1, 2, and 3 which are used primarily to test, troubleshoot, and repair assemblies and subassemblies from the RCDC and the emergency contact unit which is used to analyze HIPAR system performance and repair assemblies at the Artillery battery location. There are five positions or consoles in shop 1 and 2, and two consoles in shop 3. The consoles in shops 1 and 2 are manually operated while those in shop 3 are semiautomatic for performing test and manually operated for repair and maintenance of defective units. Each shop uses the alphanumeric system for locating stored test adapters and accessories used in performing test and maintenance on assemblies. Each console is capable of being used to test different assemblies or UUT's and master TB 9-4900-250-35/1 is used to route the UUT to the correct console. When the UUT arrives at the correct console the operator also uses the master TB to determine which manual, stored at the console, should be used to perform maintenance on the UUT. When the UUT is repaired it is returned to supply channels or returned to the Nike Artillery battery from which it came.

MMS SUBCOURSE NUMBER 151, NIKE MISSILE AND TEST EQUIPMENT

EXERCISES FOR LESSON 5

1. After performing a voltage check on a relay assembly, at what panel in shop 1 is switching accomplished to change to a relay check?

   A. A
   B. M
   C. P
   D. Z

2. Which is the first step in determining the location of a malfunction in a faulty chassis?

   A. Route to the proper console
   B. Connect the UUT to the console
   C. Visually inspect the UUT
   D. Measure the UUT parameters

3. At what location in the electrical test and maintenance table of position 1 is the receiver-gate generator stored?

   A. A1
   B. A2
   C. B1
   D. B2

4. Which test set is located at position 3 of electronic shop 1?

   A. Servo test set AN/MPM-48A
   B. Computer test set AN/MPM-45
   C. Electrical power test set AN/MPM-42
   D. Radar test set AN/MPM-37A

5. Which electronic shop position is used to test computer assemblies?

   A. 1
   B. 2
   C. 4
   D. 5

6. In what portion of shop 3 are the programmed comparator limits compared with the measured parameters from the UUT's?

   A. Digital readout circuits
   B. Digital multimeter and counter
   C. Time stretcher
   D. Waveform analyzer-monitor

7. Which gives information concerning calibration requirements for test equipment associated with the improved Nike Hercules system?

   A. TB 9-4900-250-35/1
   B. TM 9-1400-250-34/2/2
   C. TB 750-236
   D. TB 9-131-2

8. Which consoles are located in electronic shop 3?

   A. 6 and 7
   B. 4 and 5
   C. 2 and 3
   D. 1, 2, and 3

9. Which is NOT a functional group of the equipment mounted in shop 3?

   A. GFE
   B. DAME
   C. SPTE
   D. CPE

10. Which is one of the primary considerations for retaining the use of patch cards in electronic shop 3?

    A. Simple
    B. Economical
    C. Automatic
    D. Fault free

MMS 151, 5-P23

11. In the absence of a pass indication on console 7, what action should be taken on part of the operator?

    A. Perform troubleshooting procedures
    B. Tag the UUT with the step failed
    C. Place the CPE into semiautomatic operation
    D. Perform the acceptance test

12. What is a function of the console programming equipment in electronic shop 3?

    A. Select and position switches
    B. Test the UUT
    C. Establish comparator limits
    D. Verify program card selection

13. A chassis with part number 9140754 arrives at a Nike direct support unit. To which electronic shop position should this chassis be sent to receive proper testing?

    A. 1
    B. 3
    C. 4
    D. 5

14. What chapter of TM 9-1400-250-34/3/2 should be used by the technician to make an acceptance test on part number 9140767?

    A. 21
    B. 9
    C. 5
    D. 4

15. What was the primary purpose of automating the operation of electronic shop 3?

    A. Increase test accuracy
    B. Decrease test time
    C. Increase reliability
    D. Decrease equipment cost

16. What is the maximum number of tube stages mounted on a minispec?

    A. 2
    B. 3
    C. 4
    D. 5

17. In which area are the connectors for interconnections between the UUT and console 6 located?

    A. A1
    B. A2
    C. A3
    D. A4

18. A UUT being tested at console 6 does NOT meet the comparator limits established by the program. If the operator successfully performs all the prescribed troubleshooting aids and finds all switches in the correct position, to what location is the malfunction isolated?

    A. Console
    B. UUT
    C. Interconnecting cables
    D. Crossbar switch

19. Which class of information is NOT contained on the program cards for electronic shop 3?

    A. Switch position
    B. Card select
    C. End of card
    D. UUT pass or fail

20. What is one maintenance problem associated with electronic shop 3?

    A. Patch cards
    B. Crossbar switch
    C. Time interval test
    D. Card reader adjustments

21. The electrical program signals are generated by the card reader in shop 3 when the

    A. picker knite puts the card into the feed rollers.
    B. card is clamped onto the drum.
    C. star wheels drop into the punched holes.
    D. microswitches drop into the punched holes.

22. Personnel holding which MOS should be dispatched to the HIPAR with the ECU?

    A. 23N
    B. 23U
    C. 22L
    D. 22G

23. Which establishes continuity with the verification circuits in the remote switching control at console 6?

    A. Program card
    B. Patch cards
    C. Card reader
    D. Console programming equipment

24. In which alpha designated drawers of the electrical test and maintenance tables are the patch cards located?

    A. A1, A2 and B1, B2
    B. A1, A2 and C1, C2
    C. B1, B2 and C1, C2
    D. C1, C2 and D1, D2

25. Which is tested at position 2 of electronic shop 1?

    A. Relays
    B. Voltage regulators
    C. CRT indicators
    D. Communication assemblies

26. Which shop position is used to test a complete RF system?

    A. AN/MPM-43
    B. AN/MPM-37A
    C. AN/MPM-48A
    D. AN/MPM-47

27. What was added to the field maintenance test equipment to change it to an improved field maintenance system?

    A. Emergency contact unit
    B. Electronic shop 1
    C. Electronic shop 2
    D. Electronic shop 3

28. What information is contained in the last two columns of a punched card of electronic shop 3 if the test is incomplete?

    A. Card select
    B. Switch position
    C. Comparator limits
    D. End of test

29. Which is used to determine the position at which a UUT is tested?

    A. DA Form 2407
    B. TM 9-1400-250-34/2/2
    C. TB 9-4900-250-35/1
    D. Chassis control number

30. What instructions are given by the acceptance test portion of the chapter in TM 9-1400-250-34/2/2 pertaining to part number 9140712?

    A. Purpose of the test
    B. Procedures for connecting the UUT
    C. Waveshapes to be observed
    D. Test layouts to be used

LESSON 6. HERCULES INSPECTION AND MAINTENANCE CONCEPTS

MMS Subcourse No 151	Nike Missile and Test Equipment
Lesson Objective	To provide you with a general knowledge of the purpose, types, frequency, and procedures for inspecting a Nike Hercules system and maintenance concepts including MOS.
Credit Hours	Two

TEXT

1. INTRODUCTION.

a. The efficiency and adequacy of Nike support maintenance is largely determined by the sufficiency and serviceability of the Nike equipment in the possession of using units, and the rapidity and efficiency with which responsible Nike Ordnance maintenance units respond to user demands.

b. Effective ordnance support for the Nike system is a combination of the maintenance program conducted at the organizational level and the support maintenance provided by the supporting ordnance units. In effect, it is a partnership with both ordnance and the air defense artillery battalion (using unit) having definite responsibilities with regard to the supply and maintenance of TOE equipment. Neglect or inefficiency on the part of either will cast an adverse reflection on the ordnance support effort, impose demands on ordnance support in the form of unwarranted workloads, and reduce the ability of Artillery to perform its mission.

c. The Artillery is responsible for the proper care, operation, and maintenance of their TOE equipment. Supporting Nike maintenance units can materially reduce their workload by assuring that the Artillery is familiar with and are carrying out their maintenance responsibilities. It is essential that Nike Ordnance support units provide an effective technical assistance service to the Artillery in order that Artillery personnel remain proficient in the accomplishment of their duties. Similarly, supporting Nike Ordnance units must function proficiently in order to be responsive to Artillery's demands for timely and adequate supply of repair parts and prompt repair of unserviceable equipment. Therefore, frequent examinations and constant surveillance of all aspects of these responsibilities are of vital concern to all Ordnance commanders. This is accomplished largely through periodic inspections of Nike Hercules equipment in the hands of the Artillery and the inspection of supply and maintenance procedures and facilities of Artillery and supporting Ordnance units.

d. Inspections of the Nike system and related supply and maintenance operations of the Artillery are a primary responsibility of the supporting Ordnance direct support unit. These inspections will aid the Artillery by insuring their organizational maintenance is being performed properly.

2. CATEGORIES OF MAINTENANCE.

a. **Nike organizational maintenance.** Nike organizational maintenance is that maintenance normally authorized for, the responsibility of, and performed by the Air Defense Artillery on equipment in its possession. This maintenance consists of functions and repairs within the capabilities of authorized personnel, skills, tools, and test equipment as prescribed in appropriate Department of the Army TOE's or TD's. It usually includes operation, preventive maintenance, inspection, cleaning, servicing, lubricating, testing, and adjusting as prescribed and authorized in TM 9-1400-250-15/3 and the appropriate checks and adjustments technical manuals. This maintenance will include replacement of chassis and certain parts as authorized by technical manuals which have 12 P or 15 P as the last group of digits in the TM number. (Example: TM 9-1430-250-12P/2/2.) (Organizational maintenance was formerly known as first and second echelon maintenance.) Two levels of maintenance on the Nike system are performed by artillery personnel. This maintenance is accomplished by two distinct skill levels of personnel. The operator or user of the equipment carries a 16 series MOS and performs such tasks as: exercising proper care, use, operation, cleaning, preservation, and lubrication and such adjustment, minor repair, and testing and parts replacement as authorized by the operator and organizational maintenance manuals, tools, and parts list. The other level of organizational maintenance is performed by three specially trained maintenance mechanics assigned to each battery. These MOS are: Defense Acquisition Radar Mechanic (24P), Hercules Fire Control Mechanic (24Q) and Hercules Electronics Mechanic (24U). The TOE authorizes these additional skilled mechanics tools and the 12P or 15P manual authorizes additional parts for the performance of maintenance beyond the capabilities and facilities of the operator level. Maintenance exceeding the authorized organizational category may be performed by organizational maintenance personnel when authorized by the direct support commanders. The Nike direct support commanders should be assured the Artillery has the capability to perform this maintenance before authorization is given.

(1) Missile. Organizational maintenance of the missile electronic guidance section does not include component repair and extends only to replacement of the complete set of those plug-in type parts and/or subassemblies provided as organizational repair parts. The organizational maintenance on missile mechanical items extends only to replacement of parts not requiring the use of special tools or skills beyond those associated with normal missile assembly, servicing, and checkout.

(2) Ground guidance equipment. Organizational maintenance is limited to those repairs and replacements which can be accomplished by tools, test equipment, and repair parts authorized for the Artillery.

(3) Extent of repair. The degree or extent of repairs, replacements, and maintenance performed by the Artillery is limited to that specified and authorized by the appropriate technical publication (TOE or TD and the 12 P or 15 P manual). Unserviceable organizational repair parts are repaired or replaced by direct exchange with the Nike direct support platoon (fig 1), except for those having no reclaimable value (expendable-nonrecoverable).

b. Nike direct support maintenance. Direct support maintenance is the maintenance authorized and performed by the Nike direct support platoon (fig 1) in direct support of the Artillery battalion. This category is normally limited to maintenance consisting of repair or replacement of unserviceable parts, subassemblies, or assemblies. This category of maintenance is authorized by appropriate technical publications (TOE's or TD, repair parts, and special tool list) to be performed by specially trained units in direct support of Nike air defense artillery battalions. This category of maintenance is authorized a larger assortment of parts, subassemblies, and assemblies, and more precise tools and test equipment than is provided to the Artillery. Nike direct support organizations repair assemblies and subassemblies and repair the overflow from the organizational category within limits imposed by specified authorization of tools, parts, and test equipment. They also support organizational maintenance by providing technical assistance, mobile repair crews, and repair parts, when necessary.

c. **Nike general support maintenance.**

(1) General support maintenance is that level of maintenance authorized by appropriate technical publications to be performed by units organized as semimobile or permanent shops to serve the lower categories of maintenance. The principal function of general support maintenance is to repair assemblies and subassemblies for return to stock.

(2) General support embraces all assistance within the combat zone or communications zone required to back up the direct support unit. General support maintenance units are provided to receive the overflow of unserviceable materiel from a number of direct support units. These units do not normally have direct contact with Artillery and provide supply support only for organic shop operations. Their mission is to evacuate unserviceable materiel in volume from the direct support unit for repair and return it to stock with a minimum of delay and expense of evacuation and to permit the rapid displacement of the direct support unit. General support maintenance in the zone of the interior,

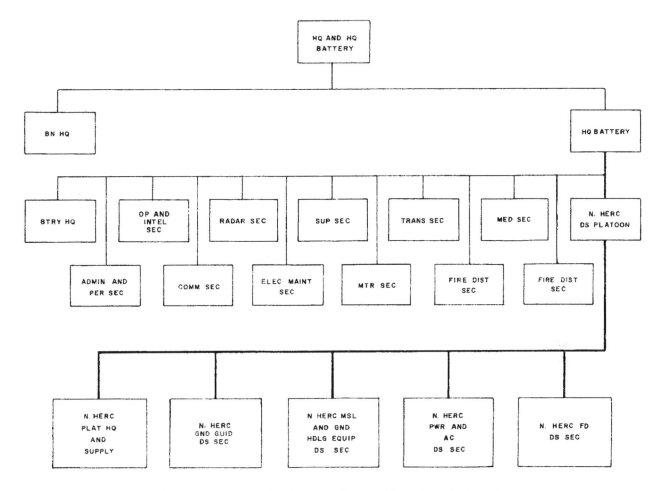

Figure 1. Headquarters and Headquarters Battery Air Defense Artillery Battalion.

if not provided by TOE's, is performed at post-ordnance level. This is usually accomplished by employment of wage board (WB) civilian personnel who possess skills equivalent to those discussed in paragraph 6.

d. Nike depot maintenance. Depot maintenance is that degree of maintenance authorized for rebuilding major items, assemblies, parts, accessories, tools, and test equipment. It normally supports supply on a rebuild and return-to-stock basis. This maintenance is performed on materiel that requires a major overhaul or the complete rebuild of parts, subassemblies, assemblies, and/or the end item, as required. An end item is a combination of components, assemblies, and/or parts which is ready for its intended use. Such maintenance is intended to increase stocks of serviceable equipment or to support lower categories of maintenance by the use of more extensive shop equipment and personnel of higher technical skills than are available in organizational or support maintenance activities.

3. MAINTENANCE ASSISTANCE AND INSTRUCTION TEAM (MAIT) PROGRAM.

a. Technical assistance is available to each category of maintenance through the Maintenance Assistance and Instruction Team (MAIT) program. Its primary purpose is to provide commanders a tool for assisting subordinate units in maintaining materiel and their units at a high state of readiness. Each team is organized from personnel resources with the technical expertise needed to assist commanders in identifying and solving maintenance problems which contribute to unacceptable materiel readiness conditions.

b. It is the responsibility of commanders at all levels to utilize MAIT and other sources available to identify and solve maintenance problems, thereby maintaining their units at a high state of readiness at all times.

c. Maintenance Assistance and Instruction Teams operate and make visits in accordance with procedures as outlined in AR 750-51. No visit is conducted unannounced. Prior arrangements are made with the unit to be visited so that proper team composition may be determined and the unit to be visited can be notified seven working days in advance. Visits are arranged as outlined below.

(1) Command directed based upon determination that assistance is required.

(2) Requested by units requiring assistance and instruction.

(3) Requested by an organization desiring assistance and instruction for its subordinate units.

d. MAIT's are organized to provide assistance and instruction in all phases of maintenance and supply and in the general areas of management, training, publications, shop layout and production, and quality control.

e. Emphasis of the visit will be to identify underlying problems in areas needing improvements and provide the "what to do" and "how to do" in those areas. No rating or score will be made of a unit. The team chief will advise the unit commander on recommended follow up actions and provide a list of problem areas.

4. ORGANIZATION OF THE NIKE BATTALION. There are several organizations which exist for the operation, use, and maintenance of the Nike equipment. It is beyond the scope of this lesson to cover each of these concepts in detail; however, the Headquarters and Headquarters Battery Air Defense Artillery Battalion, which is organized under TOE 44-536, will be covered. Its mission is to provide command, administration, supply, organizational maintenance and operation control for the air defense artillery battalion, Nike Hercules, in its surface to air and surface to surface role. This battalion commands four firing batteries, each battery being supported by the Nike direct support platoon. The organizational chart for this battalion is shown in figure 1. In this organization the Nike Hercules direct support platoon, shown by the heavy lines in figure 1, is organic to the battalion and is responsible for direct support maintenance of the Nike radars, computer, missile, launcher, and handling equipment in the four firing batteries of the battalion. It is also responsible for organizational maintenance of its own shop equipment.

5. NIKE DIRECT SUPPORT PLATOON.

a. The four Nike Hercules missile firing batteries are serviced by the Nike direct support platoon (fig 1). Nike direct support is that ordnance service (maintenance and supply) rendered the Artillery on class VII and IX materiel. The complete missile body with explosives and propellants in one or more packages is considered an ammunition item (class V) and is handled through ammunition supply channels. However, the direct support platoon performs maintenance on missiles (less the warhead). All user needs including maintenance service, supply service inspection, instruction in the proper care and handling, and assistance in operation, where required, are normal direct support functions. The direct support platoon has the capability of supplying parts and performing direct support maintenance for all Nike equipment assigned to the Air Defense Artillery missile battalion. It is equipped and trained to detect and isolate malfunctions and to perform repairs of assemblies and subassemblies in the combat zone immediately adjacent to the units supported. The Nike direct support platoon is provided transportation and its equipment is mounted in such a manner to allow it to make a move simultaneously with the battalion when given a minimum of 4 hours' notice.

b. Execution of the direct support mission through the medium of contact teams is followed to the extent practicable. Direct support platoons are organized and equipped with a supply of fast moving repair parts, organizational replacement items, and support maintenance tools to carry emergency repair service to the battery emplacement. Their repair capability is emergency in nature and includes isolation of failure to chassis-type assemblies and the replacement of unserviceable chassis with serviceable ones. Component repair, except of a minor nature, is performed at the direct support shop.

c. A direct exchange stock is maintained by the direct support platoon. From this stock certain unserviceable subassemblies and chassis in the hands of the Artillery are exchanged directly for a serviceable replacement. Unserviceable materiel not immediately repairable due to lack of time, tools, skills, or volume is evacuated to the general support maintenance unit. A maintenance float based upon known average deadline percentage is provided at the general support level for the replacement of evacuated materiel.

d. Enforcement of organizational maintenance is a command responsibility of all levels. The Nike direct support platoon unit is delegated the responsibility of performing periodic technical inspections of Nike equipment to insure its adequate care and preservation by the Artillery. It is also the responsibility of the Nike direct support platoon commander, in accordance with the assigned maintenance mission, to advise, assist, and instruct Artillery personnel in proper maintenance and supply discipline and procedures.

6. NIKE HERCULES ORDNANCE PERSONNEL.

a. **General.** Ordnance, Signal, and Engineer personnel are assigned to the Nike direct support platoon (fig 1). The platoon leader (missile maintenance officer, MOS 4516), supply, administrative, and staff personnel are assigned to the Nike Hercules platoon headquarters. Ordnance trained specialists are assigned to the Nike Hercules ground guidance DS section, and the Nike Hercules missile and handling equipment DS section (fig 1). Engineer trained personnel are assigned to the Nike Hercules power and air-conditioner DS section while Signal trained personnel are assigned to the Nike Hercules fire distribution section.

b. **Military occupational specialty (MOS).** Ordnance personnel assigned to the direct support platoon have one of the following basic MOS's: 22G20, 22L20, 22M20, 23N20, or a 23U20. Each man holding one of these MOS's must have definite skills, and there exists chains of progression which can lead him to a warrant officer MOS 251B. The prefix digits in the MOS, i.e., 22 or 23, indicates the occupational area and career group. The 22 indicates guided missile electronic maintenance and 23 indicates missile fire control electronic maintenance. The alpha character indicates the state of advancement. The "A" indicates entry level and the "B" through "Y" normally indicate advancement level. "Z" and sometimes other alpha characters in the missile field indicates a capper MOS. A capper MOS is the top progression in the chain for enlisted personnel and this MOS normally supervises two or more advanced specialists. The grade held by each of these MOS should vary with his degree of knowledge, skill, and responsibilities. The last two digits of the MOS indicate these skill levels. The grade held in each level may vary two or three steps within each MOS; i.e., personnel with a 20 skill level MOS may advance from E4 through E6 depending on his knowledge, skills, and duties. When the E6 grade foreman is reached, he has advanced to the 40 skill level and may then advance to warrant officer 251B or remain in the enlisted field and obtain the capper MOS, which is a 23W50 for the Nike Support Maintenance field. The 23W50 may be an E7 or E8 depending upon his level of proficiency and assignment. The 23W50, E7 is a Nike maintenance supervisor, while the E8 may be either a Nike maintenance chief or first sergeant.

c. **Nike Hercules missile and ground handling equipment DS section personnel.** Under TOE 44-536 this section, at full strength, consists of 22 positions which include the following MOS:

MOS	Title
251-B	Air Defense Missile System Repair Technician, Nike

Skills and Knowledges

Must know operation, function, troubleshooting procedures, repair and maintenance of AD missiles and associated ground guidance equipment, including electrical, electronic, mechanical, electromechanical, hydraulic, and hydropneumatic systems. Must know principles and utilization of special electronic test equipment. Must know theory and function of vacuum tubes, transistors, solid state devices, and associated circuits and circuit elements. Must know safety precautions to be utilized in the handling and storing of missiles, propellants, and w. heads and in working near high voltages. Must know application of advanced electronic theory and system analysis procedures in diagnosis of complex malfunctions. Must know organizational maintenance responsibilities of supported units. Must know ordnance supply channels for replacement and spare parts. Must be able to act as chief of section, detachment, or team engaged in field and depot maintenance of air defense missile systems.

MOS	Title
23W50	Nike Maintenance Chief

Skills and Knowledges

Must be qualified in a Nike maintenance MOS. Must know capabilities and limitations of maintenance equipment and subordinate personnel in order to establish workloads and repair priorities. Must know administrative procedures, command, and supply channels of unit to which assigned. Must know pertinent technical manuals, regulations, and inspection techniques applicable to Nike launcher control, radars, computers, guidance systems, and associated test equipment. Must know general shop planning and be able to recommend establishment of procedures for receipt, storage, inspection, testing, and repair of Nike system electrical and mechanical components. Must know technical mission, maintenance responsibilities, and operation of supported and supporting units. Must know function and limitations of missile system contact teams. Must know capabilities and limitations of missile repair shops attached to missile firing battalions. Must be able to organize and direct section maintenance activities to include both shop and contact team maintenance. Must be able to organize and supervise inspection and maintenance teams. Must be able to diagnose and evaluate malfunctions to determine seriousness of malfunction, length of time, tools and parts required to repair equipment or component, and whether such maintenance and repair can be accomplished by direct or general support. Must be able to coordinate maintenance activities of organizational and higher level repair personnel. Must be able to conduct on-the-job training programs. Must be able to apply sound management principles, coordinate repair activities, and maintain a high level of unit cooperation and productivity. Must be able to provide technical guidance to maintenance personnel performing complex repairs on missile equipment. Must be able to supervise modification of equipment and provide on-the-job maintenance training of modified equipment. Must be able to read and utilize TOE, TD, TA, and supply manuals.

MOS	Title
22G	Nike Launcher System Repairman

Skills and Knowledges

22G20. Must know nomenclature, location of components, function, theory, and operating procedures of the Nike launcher system electrical, electronic, and mechanical equipment and associated test equipment. Must know maintenance procedures for all associated field maintenance test equipment and field maintenance special test equipment. Must know inspection and maintenance procedures for Nike launcher system electrical, electronic, and mechanical equipment. Must know repair and replacement procedures. Must be able to adjust and test repaired components or combinations of components. Must be able to apply electrical, electronic, and mechanical theory, and system analysis procedures in diagnosis and isolation of malfunctions, operation, adjustments, and field maintenance repair of mechanical type IV test equipment, except field maintenance electronic test equipment. Must be able to interpret electronic and electrical schematic diagrams, mechanical system diagrams, and understand pertinent technical literature. Must be able to use electrician's and mechanic's common and special handtools.

22G40. Must be qualified as Nike Launcher System Repairman 22G20. Must know general shop planning and be able to recommend establishment of procedures for receipt, storage, inspection, testing, and repair on Nike launcher system electrical, electronic, and mechanical components, and know the capabilities and limitations of maintenance equipment and subordinate personnel in order to establish workload priorities. Must know how to organize and supervise inspection and maintenance teams.

MOS	Title
22M	Nike Missile Repairman

Skills and Knowledges

22M20. Must know nomenclature, function, and operation of Nike missile electronic field maintenance test equipment. Must know organizational and field maintenance of Nike missile test equipment. Must know operation and adjustments of field maintenance mechanical and hydraulic test equipment and the procedures necessary to perform final checkout of repaired Nike missiles. Must know organizational maintenance and inspection procedures pertinent to the Nike missile. Must know organizational maintenance in order to instruct operating and organizational maintenance personnel. Must be able to repair and replace all Nike missile components and structural assemblies. Must be able to apply electronic theory and system analysis in diagnosis and isolation malfunctions. Must be able to understand pertinent technical publications and interpret electronic circuitry diagrams. Must be able to apply modification work orders pertaining to the missile test equipment, organizational maintenance equipment, and Nike missiles. Must be able to use electrician's and mechanic's common handtools.

22M40. Must be qualified as Nike Missile Repairman 22M20. Must know general shop planning, procedures for receipt, storage, inspection, test, and repair of Nike missile components. Must know capabilities and limitations of maintenance equipment and subordinate personnel. Must be able to inspect, instruct, and report on the status of organizational maintenance of Nike missiles.

d. **Miscellaneous personnel in the ground handling DS section.** Additional MOS allotted to this section are Missile Mechanical Repair Apprentice 46A and Power Generation Specialist 52B. The 52B MOS performs organizational and higher level maintenance and repair on portable generator sets and frequency converters equipped with electric motors, diesel, gasoline, or gas turbine engines.

e. **Nike Hercules ground guidance DS section personnel.** This section is allotted a warrant officer 251B, an enlisted capper MOS 23W, an apprentice 22A, and power generation specialist as described in paragraphs 6c and d. The main work functions of this section, however, are performed by the personnel having the following MOS and skills.

MOS	Title
22L	Nike Test Equipment Repairman

Skills and Knowledges

22L20. Must know operation, inspection, testing, comparison, adjustment, repair, nomenclature, and organizational and field maintenance procedures for Nike electronics shop 1, 2, and 3. Must know how to test, compare, adjust, repair, and perform field maintenance of all chassis and electronic test equipment checked in these shops. Must be able to apply electronic theory and system analysis procedures in diagnosis and isolation of malfunctions. Must be able to apply modification work orders applicable to Nike electronics shops. Must be able to understand pertinent technical publications and use electrician's and mechanic's common and special handtools.

22L40. Must be qualified as Nike Test Equipment Repairman 22L20. Must know general shop planning and procedures for receipt, storage, inspection, testing, and repair of using unit test equipment. Must know capabilities and limitations of maintenance equipment and subordinate personnel in order to establish workloads and repair priorities. Must know administrative procedures and command and supply channels of unit to which assigned.

MOS	Title
23N	Nike Track Radar Repairman

Skills and Knowledges

23N20. Must know nomenclature, construction, components, function, theory, and operating procedures of Nike LOPAR, TTR, TRR, MTR, and computer pertinent to repair or removal of faulty parts, components, and adjustment and alinement of repaired components. Must know operation and adjustment of test equipment. Must know inspection and maintenance procedures for Nike LOPAR, TTR, TRR, MTR, computer, and associated test equipment. Must be able to apply electronic theory and system analysis procedures for diagnosis and isolation of malfunctions. Must be able to interpret electronic schematic diagrams and understand pertinent technical literature. Must be able to use electrician's common and special handtools.

23N40. Must be qualified as Nike Radar Repairman 23N20. Must know general shop planning and procedures for receipt, storage, inspection, testing, and repair of Nike LOPAR, TTR, TRR, MTR, and computer components, and combination of components. Must know administrative and supply procedures. Must be able to instruct subordinates in on-the-job training programs. Must know capabilities of maintenance equipment and subordinate personnel in order to establish workload priorities.

MOS	Title
23U	Nike HIPAR-Simulator Repairman

Skills and Knowledges

23U20. Must know nomenclature, location of components, function, theory, and operating procedures of Nike HIPAR, radar target simulator, and associated organizational maintenance equipment and test equipment for isolation of faulty parts or components. Must know operation and adjustment of test equipment. Must know inspection and maintenance procedures for Nike HIPAR, radar target simulator, and associated test equipment. Must be able to apply electronic theory and system analysis procedures for diagnosis and isolation of malfunctions. Must be able to modify equipment in accordance with modification work orders. Must be able to use electrician's common and special handtools.

23U40. Must be qualified as Nike HIPAR-Simulator Repairman 23U20. Must know general shop planning and procedures for receipt, storage, inspection, testing, and repair of Nike HIPAR and radar target simulator. Must know administrative and supply procedures. Must know capabilities of maintenance equipment and subordinate personnel. Must be able to instruct subordinates in on-the-job training programs.

f. **Nike Hercules platoon headquarters and supply personnel.** The platoon is led by a Missile Maintenance Officer 4516. Various other positions are allotted the platoon headquarters which include supply specialists, administrative (clerical) personnel, wheeled vehicle mechanics, and a cook.

7. ARTILLERY BATTALION MAINTENANCE INSPECTIONS.

a. **Purpose of inspections.** Inspections serve many purposes, the most important of which are to assist Artillery commanders in determining the ability of units to perform their assigned missions; inform commanders of the condition of materiel in the hands of troops; inform commanders of the adequacy and efficiency of supply and maintenance operations, and the ability of personnel performing these duties; improve relations and confidence between Artillery and supporting Ordnance units; assist in predicting future maintenance and supply requirements; aid in detecting impending failures in equipment before unserviceability results; aid in determining the need for improvements in training, procedures, organization, or equipment; and provide a basis for making decisions.

b. **Types of Inspection.**

(1) Introduction. Inspections include tactical and training, annual general, command, spot check, and technical inspections. The Command Maintenance Management Inspection (CMMI) has been replaced by the Maintenance Assistance and Instruction Team Program (MAIT). The MAIT, as discussed in para 3, is not to be considered an inspection, rather an aid to commanders in evaluating their maintenance program.

(2) Tactical and training inspections. These inspections are used to improve combat efficiency, to determine the state of training and the degree of operational readiness of the inspected units, to remove obstacles to training, and generally to further the Department of the Army training program.

(3) Annual general inspections. These inspections, provided for by AR 20-1, are performed by inspectors general acting under the special instructions of major commanders. They are conducted on a yearly basis and cover the administrative, operational, logistic, tactical, and security portions of the unit being inspected. For the unit in the field, the basic purpose of annual general inspections is to insure high standards of discipline, efficiency, and economy.

(4) Command inspections. Actually, all inspections are a command function as they are conducted under command authority. However, one characteristic of a command inspection is that the commander personally particapates. Command inspections are performed on an annual basis, however, they may be conducted as frequently as the commander believes it to be necessary. The commander is assisted by an inspection team composed of staff members, technical assistants, or both if appropriate. These inspections may be conducted "formally" by giving advance notice and using an established inspection procedure; or they may be "informal" by inspecting a unit at any opportune time and place without a set procedure. These inspections are a valuable aid in determining the efficiency of the preventive maintenance program; in determining whether mess, supply, administrative and maintenance procedures meet prescribed standards; in determining whether equipment is serviceable and whether it is being used properly; in evaluating the efficiency of operations; in determining whether directives and established procedures are being complied with; and in determining the operational readiness of personnel and equipment. DA Pam 750-1 provides valuable information for the conduct of preventive maintenance inspections. AR 220-1 provides commanders at all levels with a uniform method of evaluating serviceability of equipment issued to units.

(5) Spot-check inspection. A spot-check inspection is an informal type of inspection and is not required by Army Regulations, however, it is frequently used by commanders to determine the adequacy and effectiveness of their organizational maintenance. Spot-check inspections are performed by technically qualified personnel and the equipment is inspected wherever it is used (roadside, motor park, training area, etc.). This type of inspection will provide the commander with an indication of the day-to-day condition of his units equipment. It will also provide the following information:

(a) Availability of required publications.

(b) Accuracy of supply records and supply procedures.

(c) Supply economy practices.

(d) Care of tools and equipment.

(e) Status of authorized stock levels of equipment and repair parts.

(6) Technical inspections. These inspections are performed on major items of equipment to determine their physical condition and, if necessary, to recommend corrective action. Technical inspections are always performed by qualified maintenance personnel. Technical inspection of equipment is normally performed

under the following circumstances:

    (a) Upon acceptance of the equipment from the factory.

    (b) Upon receipt of equipment at each level down to the user or operator.

    (c) When there is a change of command, to prevent erroneous fixing of responsibility.

    (d) Whenever equipment is turned in to a support shop for repair or modification.

8. **SUMMARY.** This lesson covered the categories of maintenance for the Nike system and some of the duties and responsibilities of personnel trained to discharge these duties. At the organizational level there are the 16 series MOS's which are the crewmen or operators of the Nike system and the 24P, Q, and U who are the maintenance mechanics. These personnel are trained to perform organizational maintenance on the fire control, missile, and launcher equipment. The enlisted support maintenance personnel are assigned to the direct support platoon and hold MOS's 22A, 22G, 22L, 22M, 23N, 23U, and 23W. Also assigned to this platoon are the Warrant Officer 251B, Air Defense Missile System Repair Technician, Nike and the MOS 4516 Missile Maintenance Officer. This lesson also dealt with inspections and the Maintenance and Assistance Instruction Team (MAIT). Inspections are a valuable tool for informing commanders as to the condition of their men and materiel, while MAIT provides expert and valuable assistance in correcting any supply or maintenance problem.

MMS SUBCOURSE NUMBER 151, NIKE MISSILE AND TEST EQUIPMENT

EXERCISES FOR LESSON 6

1. Which would be a primary cause of unwarranted workloads being imposed on a Nike direct support maintenance unit?

   A. Inadequate organizational maintenance
   B. Inadequate supply of direct support repair parts
   C. Untrained ordnance personnel
   D. Inadequate general support

2. Under which condition should a Nike direct support commander authorize the Artillery to perform maintenance which falls within the direct support category?

   A. Never
   B. When the DS sections are overworked
   C. When the Artillery has the capability
   D. When the artillery wants to perform the maintenance

3. Which is NOT a function of Nike organizational maintenance?

   A. Inspecting
   B. Adjusting
   C. Replacing parts
   D. Rebuild

4. What should be done with overflow work at the Nike direct support level?

   A. Backlogged
   B. Evacuated to general support
   C. Evacuated to depot
   D. Performed by organizational

5. Which maintenance should be performed by the Artillery on the electronic guidance section of the Nike Hercules missile?

   A. Component repair
   B. Components requiring special tools
   C. Plug-in type replacement parts or subassemblies
   D. Replacement of parts associated with assembly, servicing, and checkout

6. Which MOS is the Artillery's Hercules fire control mechanic?

   A. 23N
   B. 24P
   C. 24Q
   D. 24U

7. Which category of maintenance has the primary mission to evacuate unserviceable materiel, repair it, and return it to stock?

   A. Organizational
   B. Direct support
   C. General support
   D. Depot

8. Which technical assistance is provided under the provision of Army Regulation 750-51?

   A. Manufacturer's representatives
   B. Maintenance assistance and instruction team
   C. Regional maintenance representatives
   D. Contract field technicians

9. Most component repair performed by the Nike direct support platoon is performed at which location?

   A. Nike installation
   B. Emergency contact unit
   C. Electronic shop 3
   D. Direct support shop

10. What is indicated by the prefix digits of the enlisted personnel MOS?

    A. Occupational area and career group
    B. Skill level and job specialty
    C. Advancement level
    D. Entry level

11. The 23U MOS is responsible for support maintenance on which equipment?

    A. HIPAR and radar target simulator
    B. LOPAR and computer
    C. TTR, TRR, and MTR
    D. Launcher electrical and mechanical

NOW AVAILABLE!

NASA PROJECT GEMINI

FAMILIARIZATION MANUAL
Manned Satellite Capsule

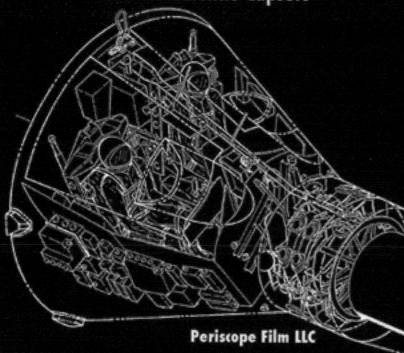

Periscope Film LLC

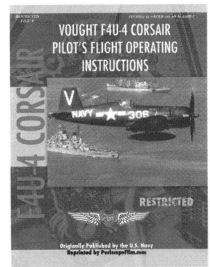
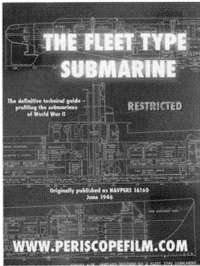
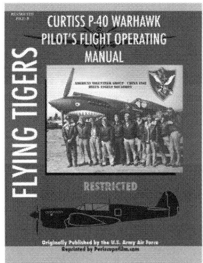
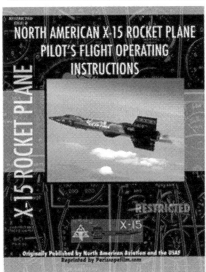
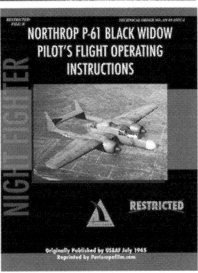

ALSO NOW AVAILABLE
FROM PERISCOPEFILM.COM

©2011 Periscope Film LLC
All Rights Reserved
ISBN #978-1-937684-92-1
www.PeriscopeFilm.com

Made in the USA
San Bernardino, CA
14 May 2016